THE LAND OF THE ENGLISH PEOPLE

Portraits of the Nations Series

THE LAND

of the

ENGLISH PEOPLE

BY ALICIA STREET

𝔓ortraits of the 𝔑ations 𝔖eries

J. B. LIPPINCOTT COMPANY
PHILADELPHIA AND NEW YORK

COPYRIGHT, 1946, 1953, BY ALICIA STREET

Revised 1963
Fourth Printing

Printed in the United States of America

Library of Congress catalog card number 53-5429

To John

Contents

Illustrations, from photographs, and map grouped in signatures following pages 66 and 98

Foreword

WHEN the Second World War was well under way and both American and British writers were doing their best to introduce us to each other on a more realistic basis than movies could afford, I came upon a book that did more for this than all the rest together. It was *U.S.A. at Work and Play*, by Alicia Street, whom up to that time I had known only as editor of *The Outpost*—a newsletter published by Americans in Britain to tell the folks back home about conditions there, and as chairman of the London circle of *Books Across the Sea*. This book of hers told English people what they wanted to know about the everyday life of American people, and what this life meant to them, and why; I was constantly surprised to find it telling me, an American of long standing—about as far back as we go—something true about my people that I had not realized, or the meaning of something I had taken for granted.

So when a series I have always admired—*Portraits of the Nations* —reached Britain, and I found its portrait would be drawn by Alicia Street, I knew it could not be in better hands. An American girl, born in Wakefield, Michigan, graduate of Lawrence, studying at the Sorbonne when she met the young Englishman to whom she is happily married, she has long known that sharing the same language does not altogether do away with need for an interpreter. During this war, first for civilian groups and then under the army education plan, Mrs. Street not only lectured about America to the British and—as by this time Britain was crowded with American soldiers—about England to the Americans, but also answered the countless questions asked by both sides. When she came to this country for a brief visit to her parents, I had the privilege of hearing at first hand of many such experiences. She knows what each side needs to know about the other and——even harder to tell without this particular experience——what it wants to know. Besides, she can tell it in terms of the questioner's experience.

Much as I had expected of this book, however, I was unprepared for the degree to which a great need had been filled, and the extent to which my expectations were exceeded. I have been going back and forth to Britain ever since I was twenty, for years past carrying on my work as Reader's Guide of the *Herald Tribune* from a London address as well known to my readers as that of the New York office. I have taken Britain on foot, year after year, mile after mile of ever-changing, never-failing loveliness, and more than once have crossed for Christmas. I find in this book—and this is why it so moves me—not only the England I know, but deep understanding that simply presents it. I find, as part of it, the story of the English people with few names or dates, but with that sense of continuity that means English history. Here is England as an American knows it today, drawing strength from the past, looking fearlessly into the future.

MAY LAMBERTON BECKER

CHAPTER ONE

The Country and Its Climate

WHEN Americans say "Europe" they usually mean not only that continent itself but also the two islands which lean out from its western side into the North Atlantic Ocean. They are surprised when they hear people who live on those islands speaking of Europe as something quite apart from the British Isles, saying Britain has this and Europe that, or Britain needs this and Europe something else. The surprise is natural because Americans remember that at its narrowest point the English Channel which lies between Britain and the Continent is only twenty-one miles wide. They know that the British Isles were actually a part of the Continent at an early period in the earth's history. They recall that all of the warriors who swept across Europe hundreds of years ago—the Celts, the Romans, the Teutons, the Danes, succeeded in reaching Britain. And although the sea protected Britain from Napoleon's invasion in 1803 and Hitler's invasion in 1940, her waters failed again and again to daunt young men or women who escaped from the Nazis in Holland, Belgium or France by crossing the Channel in motor or even row-boats. True, it was a dangerous journey, for the winds and currents in the Channel are notoriously strong. No one will ever know how many people were lost during such attempts to reach England. But successful escapes and the withdrawal of the British Army from Dunkirk bear sharp witness to Britain's nearness to Europe, even without the development of air power which knows no ocean barriers.

Still, though Britain is clearly a part of Europe, the history of the British Isles has not been the same as the history of the Continent and it is easy to understand why the British feel that in some ways they are outside Europe. Because they lived on islands, and were free from easy invasion, they had a better chance to live their own lives and to develop their own traditions without interruption than did the countries across the Channel. The last invasion of Britain took place in 1066, nearly nine hundred years ago. Since that time, if the British have been at war with other countries, they have fought chiefly at sea, for the sea was the great outer defensework of their country. Until the air raids of the wars of 1914–18 and 1939–45, the British people suffered little from war and had a chance to grow in number and in wealth. Naturally some of the ideas they developed were different from those of the people on the mainland, and the more different they were the more the British felt themselves to be a united and un-European people.

The larger of the two British Isles is known as Britain, and the people who live on it are, like the Americans, a mixture of many races. It contains three nations, England, Scotland and Wales, and the people of each are a product of the blending of several strains. However, the mixing took place over a very much longer period of time than it has in the United States. Furthermore, certain sections of the population are less mixed than others; for instance, the Welsh and the Scots. Their parts of the island were difficult for strangers to reach and people there remained unfriendly to outsiders. In other areas, the waves of newcomers from the Continent settled down among the local people, married among them and became a part of the English melting pot.

So Britain today is inhabited by three different peoples. First there are the two million Welsh, of Iberian and Celtic stock, who preserve their own language and customs to this day. Then there are five million Scots, a mixture of Celtic and Norse, whose capital city, Edinburgh, is one of the most beautiful in the world. Finally there are nearly forty million English, who are a product of a little Celtic stock mixed with Roman, Anglo-Saxon, Danish and Norman blood, with smaller additions of French Huguenot, Flemish and other European peoples.

Although only about three times as many people live in the United States as in England, Scotland and Wales combined, the United States is nearly thirty-four times as large as the island of Britain. Britain is only a little more than half the size of California. It is triangular in shape, its eastern side from the northern point called John O' Groats to Dover, Kent, measuring only five hundred and fifty miles, while the southern side from Dover to Land's End, Cornwall, measures three hundred and twenty miles. England and Wales taken together are about the same size as the state of Georgia. No place in Britain is more than seventy-five miles from the sea; even in the most inland sections farmers often look up to see flocks of sea-gulls wheeling over their plowed fields and say to themselves, "High winds at sea since the birds come inland; God help the sailors in their ships."

But although the British, and more particularly the English, are crowded very closely together in a very small country with smaller natural resources than the United States, there is one respect in which they are very fortunate. That is in their climate. This is perhaps a surprising statement because almost everyone has heard how annoying the weather usually is in England. Because of the frequent clouds and the moisture that hangs in the air even on fairly clear days, England has less sunshine than most countries, and its sunlight is weaker than in other places where the air is dry and clear. What is worse, the sunshine rarely lasts long enough for a person to have time to enjoy it. The weather changes constantly. If it is raining when you get up in the morning and you put on a raincoat and rubbers when you go out, the sun is almost sure to be shining by lunch time, and the raincoat and rubbers will seem a nuisance. But if you go out without them after lunch, you will probably be caught in a shower by four o'clock. Picnics ought to be fun in England because there is so much beautiful scenery and almost no mosquitoes. Instead they are often disappointing because although the day may have been bright and warm when you packed your lunch, a chilly drizzle is likely to be setting in just when you are ready to eat it. To add to the difficulties of the weather forecasters, a day in January may be as warm as a warm day in July, and a day in July may be as cold as the coldest day in January.

But although English weather is as troublesome as any in the world, the English climate—meaning average weather—is a good one. After all, there are many places in the world where Nature seems to fight against men—where rivers overflow their banks, where cyclones and hurricanes tear away towns, where plagues of insects destroy crops, where men die of extremes of heat or of cold. By comparison with these, Nature is very kind in England. What men have made during the past two thousand years has been as safe from the violence of her fiercest moods as from the violence of land warfare. Earthquakes have not leveled the ancient cathedrals nor have tornadoes uprooted the trees in the century-old orchards. In dozens of little ways the mildness of the climate affects daily life. Men ride to work on bicycles all through the year. Houses do not need storm windows for winter or screens for summer. English gardens contain yuccas and begonias, and along the south coast, even occasional palm trees. Wheat is often planted in the fall and most of the plowing is done in mid-winter. Cattle rarely have to be kept in their barns.

Obviously, English winters are seldom very cold and conversely, the summers are seldom hot. Whereas at a given point in the United States, the temperature may range from 5 below zero in the winter to 100° F. in the summer, the change at a given point in England is likely to be from 30° to 80° F. Naturally, anything above 70° is called a heat-wave, and if the temperature of a room approaches 68° people are likely to rush about opening windows and doors to let a breath of cool air into the place.

The most celebrated feature of English weather, the London fog, is very much exaggerated in reputation. Many sections of the United States have far more fog than England, and what makes a London fog thick is not so much the moisture in the air as the soot from millions of coal fires. Fortunately bad fogs are really infrequent in London. In the course of several years' residence there, I have only once been caught in a fog so thick that for a long time I could not find my way home. The people who gave London its reputation for fog were the writers of fiction who discovered that a "pea-souper" made a weird and exciting background for a story. London housewives who have to wash all their curtains after a real fog are glad that most London fogs exist only in the story books.

But it is not only the frequency of the London fog that is exaggerated; it is the quantity of rain in England. England seems to have a great deal of rain because there are so many showers. But usually very little rain falls at a time; often the rain is hardly more than a floating mist in which you can walk for hours without getting really wet. Once in a while the sky opens and there is a downpour lasting ten minutes, but in most parts of England it soon dwindles into the usual drizzle. Western Scotland is another matter. New York has forty-three and Chicago thirty-three inches of rainfall per year. Areas of heavy rainfall in western England have about sixty; London averages about twenty-five. No section of Britain is dry like the American desert but if there is a period as long as two weeks without rain farmers become very seriously worried about this "drought." They know that with such a light rainfall there can be very little water stored in the soil to carry the crops over a long period of dry weather. But they do not often have such cause for worry.

The most astonishing thing about the English climate is that it exists in an area which lies so far to the North. England lies directly across the ocean, not from the United States, but from icy Labrador. How strange is the contrast between Canada's Arctic blizzards and the winds that blow lightly across English gardens where roses bloom until Christmas time. What is the magic source of the warmth which gives the British Isles their beauty and their wealth?

It is the Gulf Stream, that mysterious great warm river that flows through the ocean. The Gulf Stream flows in a northeasterly direction, bringing warmth to the islands in the North Atlantic and making their climate so different from that of Labrador or even that of the continent of Europe. The winds that blow off the Gulf Stream keep Britain warm in the winter and cool in the summer. Once in a while a storm blowing down from the Arctic and over the cold North Sea may sweep over England's green fields, but again from the south and the west comes the warmth that soon melts snow and ice and brings back to life the frost-nipped vegetation. The Gulf Stream is Britain's best friend for the wind that blows over its warm blue waters is really the breath of life to the people who live in the British Isles.

CHAPTER TWO

The Beautiful Southern Counties

THERE is one thrill which you can never expect to have while you are in England. That is the thrill of standing on new territory and thinking, "Probably no other person has ever been here before." Such places are becoming very rare even in the New World; it is hundreds of years since the last far corner of Britain was made familiar to man.

Instead of having the thrill of making new discoveries, a visitor to England soon begins to have the very different but equally pleasant feeling that he is taking his place in a long line of people who, in all the ages of history, have stood where he stands and admired the scene before him as he is admiring it now. Early Britons with their skin painted blue, Roman soldiers, the fierce Anglo-Saxons, blond sea-faring Danes, Normans from France, and all their descendants have stood and looked at this land and loved it. Then they have gone to work to make it even more beautiful than it was before.

It is a land that is easy to love. The long summer days of the far North and the warm moist winds that blow in from the ocean give Britain a wealth of lovely trees, flowers and birds. During a great part of the year forty or fifty kinds of wildflowers can be found in blossom at one time, in the spring the list runs into hundreds. Poets have taken delight in praising the more spectacular ones. Wordsworth described

> "a crowd,
> A host of golden daffodils;
> Beside the lake, beneath the trees,
> Fluttering and dancing in the breeze."

Keats wrote of the

> "White hawthorn, and the pastoral eglantine;
> Fast-fading violets covered up in leaves."

May day songs describe one of the best loved of all English flowers, the pale yellow primrose, lightly scented and holding in its five wide-open petals the misty radiance of the English spring. After the primroses come the cowslips—not the flowers called cowslips in the United States and king-cups in England, but the English cowslips, with scented clusters of tiny yellow bells on their slender stems. Then there are the tall graceful bluebells that grow so thickly on the floor of the forest that the trees seem to stand in the blue waters of a lake.

Flowers grow everywhere in England. Along the edges of wheat fields grow wildflowers that live in American gardens:—purple foxgloves, white pansies, small as the tip of a finger, red poppies, wild peas, sturdy marigolds. On the high hills the grass is strewn with flowers that grow close to the earth—purple and white violets, eyebrights, deep blue veronicas, little yellow flowers called eggs-and-bacon. Even the ugly craters of England's bombed cities were soon made beautiful by dozens of kinds of wildflowers.

And over all the beauty of the flowers and of the blossoming trees there is always in England the song of birds. First in the spring comes the cuckoo, for whom a song was written seven hundred years ago, a song that has come down in its strange old spelling to this very day:

> "Sumer is icumen in
> Lude sing Cuckoo!"

But by the time summer really has come, the cuckoo seems to develop a sore throat, for he sings his two notes more and more hoarsely and off-key. Then the song of the sky-lark seems more beautiful than ever, as it goes endlessly on, shrill and very sweet, spilling over in ripples and trills that pour down from the sky where the bird is circling too high for the eye to see. Then there are the songs of the chaffinch and the nightingale, and though his song is not so sweet, some people choose the robin as their favorite bird—the fat little English robin after whom the American robin was named because he too had a cheerful red breast even though he did not belong to the same bird family.

One of the reasons why the English countryside is so beautiful is that fields are usually fenced not with bare wire or log fences, but with hedges of hazel or hawthorn. Hedges take more room than fences and have to be trimmed down carefully every year to make them grow very thick rather than wide and bushy; otherwise cattle could easily go through them. Then too, they take a long time to grow. All this makes them rather expensive. However, the British feel that a well-tended hedge does far more than a barbed-wire fence: it provides a nesting place for birds; it serves as a windbreak; in case of exceptionally heavy rain the hedgeroots take up the extra water and keep it from washing away seeds or soil.

People in England love all of these features of their landscape very deeply. Most of the English live in large cities and the number of farmers in England is very small in proportion to the population. But even the city-dwellers have "green fingers" which can coax an ailing plant to grow, and a little garden in which to grow it. Numbers of young city workers spend their vacations taking agricultural courses in which part of their time is spent in listening to lectures on scientific farming and part in working on the fields. Stiff backs and aching muscles do not stop it from being fun. Even though the prosperity of the 1950's resulted in a remarkable increase in the number of cars on the roads, cycling, hiking and bird-watching clubs continue to flourish and, as always, peak-hour radio and television time is frequently given to nature and gardening programs. In spite of Britain's uncertain weather, there has also been a steady increase in camping in tents, trailers or converted minibuses.

Perhaps the British love of the island on which they live is a natural result of the effort they have given to the improvement of their country. Frank Dobie, the cowboy-professor from Texas, has said that there are two kinds of landscape which are very beautiful and very satisfying: a landscape which is completely untouched by man and a landscape which has been worked upon so long that it has been brought to its finest perfection by the efforts of man. Most sections of the United States and some sections of Britain are lost somewhere between the two. Men have chopped down the original forests and mined the mountains without attempting to give the scene a new kind of beauty to replace that which they have ruined.

But although the forests which covered most parts of England disappeared long ago, the scars which were left by their destruction have also had time to go. Instead there are old fields and old pastures, surrounded by green hedges in the South, by ancient stone walls in the North, with sleepy winding brooks spanned by old stone bridges, and with scattered groves of gnarled oak trees planted, perhaps, by a farmer of five hundred years ago to provide shade for his cattle. Farmhouses built from materials that were easiest to obtain on the spot—rough stone where stone is plentiful, brick where brick-clay is at hand, with thatched roofs where the reeds grow for the thatch and slate roofs near the slate quarries—such houses fit naturally into the landscape because the materials of which they were made are already a part of it. A long time ago one man planted an orchard; his heir added a high-walled garden on a slope that caught the sun; his great-grandson had a lily-pond built where the water would mirror ivied walls and flowering trees.

So generation after generation has added its bit to the beauty of the English scene. Some men made mistakes in judgment but time itself has been kind and has softened the effect of their errors. For instance, in the late 1700's, it became the fashion for rich people to have artificial ruins, in imitation of the ruined temples of Greece and Rome, built to decorate their estates. A brand-new ruin is almost a contradiction in terms, and a row of new broken pillars must have looked very odd indeed at the time. But now that age has darkened the stone and moss has grown over the bases of the columns, the ruins look real and have a degree of charm.

There is, perhaps, another reason why English people love their land so deeply. That is the great variety of scene which is contained in this little island. England's scenery changes not only from county to county, but often within very much smaller distances. It is, in fact, a miniature version of the scenery of America or Europe. True, you must go to Scotland to find the fiords and the midnight sun of Alaska or Norway but already in northern England there are lakes and steep fields reminiscent of Vermont or New Hampshire. People who admire the beauty of the Appalachians or the Adirondacks find the mountains of Wales, Cumberland and Scotland surprisingly impressive. Not very high, they are rugged and craggy, and although people who do not mind walking fifteen or twenty miles a day can easily climb them, they usually have to start from sea-level and even thirty-five hundred feet seems a long way up.

As different as can be is the scenery in another section of England where the flat fields lie below sea-level and have to be protected by dykes. This region is, in fact, called "The Parts of Holland" because it is so much like the land across the Channel.

So it happens that a traveler through Britain is brought to a stop again and again by a wholly delightful reminder of places he has known far away—of a French fishing village or of the tawny hills of Spain or of the rolling dairy country of Wisconsin. Again and again the narrow winding roads run around a corner or over a hill to reveal a scene quite different from that passed three minutes ago.

Nor is this variety merely a matter of casual appearances. It exists in the very rock and soil of which the island consists. In some parts of the world, the rise and fall of the earth's surface or the forward movement of the great glaciers of the Ice Ages buried or swept away the original features of the area. But in Britain each changing period in the history of the earth left behind it traces of what had happened without destroying the record of earlier ages.

With all its variety, Britain can nevertheless be divided into two sections, the Highland and the Lowland. If you draw a line from the mouth of the Tees River on the northeast coast of England to the mouth of the Exe River, which runs out at the western end of the south coast, you have most of Highland Britain to the left of your line and most of Lowland Britain to the right. Taking England, Scotland and Wales together, six times as many people live in or on the edges of the Lowland area as in the stony Highlands.

The use of the word "Lowland" means only that in general the land is low-lying, not that there are no hills east of the line from the Tees to the Exe. On the contrary, some of the most famous hills in England are found in the Lowland area. These are the hills surprisingly called Downs—the North and South Downs of the counties of Kent, Surrey and Sussex. When the English call a hill a "down" they are not referring to directions at all; the word "down" really means "hill" and comes from an old word brought to England by the Anglo-Saxons twelve hundred years ago.

But the word "down" is used only in speaking of a very special kind of hill—a hill consisting largely of chalk—the stuff we write with on the blackboard, although it is not quite so white and clean when it is dug out of the quarries. Although few crops grow well in a chalky soil, it does produce short grass on which sheep are pastured, something in the chalk giving them unusually fine wool. Where the bare grassy downs meet the sea, they break off suddenly in the celebrated white cliffs which are found not only near Dover but all along the south coast of England. To walk along the springing turf of the South Downs, with the sparkling sea seven or eight hundred feet below on one side and on the other the lovely green valley called the Weald, with its farms and hedged fields and ancient stone churches, is to learn that walking in such a place is not merely a form of exercise but part of a thrilling emotional experience. Because the British enjoy walking, the general lack of roads along the top of the Downs is considered a real advantage.

West of the North and South Downs with the farming valley of the Weald between them, is another chalky area almost surrounding Southampton, the seaport through which many Americans first enter England. Southampton is not built on chalk but on lower ground. Her harbor is completely protected by the diamond-shaped Isle of Wight, an island which seems to contain in its area, roughly twenty miles by fifteen, examples of the finest scenery in the south of England. The importance of Southampton is partly due to the Isle of Wight, for the ocean tides come in from both sides of the island, making a double tide and an unusually long period of "slack water" when the tide is neither coming in nor going out and enormous ocean liners can be moved slowly into their berths.

Where the chalk rises again outside Southampton, the scene is not like the steep downs of Surrey, Sussex and Kent. Instead there is a high rolling plateau which looks as if it ought to make good land for farming, but which is, in many places, useless for that purpose because the soil is so poor. Here, on these stretches of waste land, the British have for generations had their military training grounds, and here Salisbury Plain was the only part of England that thousands of American soldiers had time to know before they sailed across the dark Channel for the invasion of France.

Still farther to the west, beyond the lush green valleys of Dorset, Somerset and Wiltshire, is another group of hills, called the Mendips. English tourists delight in visiting the romantic chasm called the Cheddar Gorge and its mysterious limestone caves, though Americans find the latter small and unimpressive by comparison with the Mammoth Caves of Kentucky.

Not far from the Mendips is Bristol, a city built on the Avon River and full of memories of the great sailing days, when John Cabot left Bristol Harbor in 1497, on his voyage to the New World, and when four-masters came in with their first cargoes from the American colonies—tobacco, indigo, rice and furs. A westward-looking city of hills, like San Francisco, beautiful despite the devastation it suffered during the air-raids of 1941, Bristol still receives shipping from North and South America.

CHAPTER THREE

East Anglia and the Midlands

SINCE the area of the United States is very great, it does not seem strange to Americans that people who live in various parts of the country speak somewhat differently from each other. It is to be expected that a New York accent is unlike a Texan one since the two states are very far apart. What does seem astonishing to Americans is the discovery that there are far more and far greater differences of accent and of dialect on the island of Britain than there are in the whole United States. Although people read the same newspapers and listen to the same voices on the radio and in the movies, they continue to use words which are remembered only locally, to give their own pronunciations to others, and, among the folk who have not had much schooling, to take liberties with English grammar which are unheard of even among the immigrants who have only recently learned English in America. A Cornish and a Yorkshire shepherd can hardly understand each other; neither can a London Cockney and a Liverpool Scotch-Irish policeman. "Heeste ye beck!" says the Aberdeen house-wife as she bids a guest farewell. "Haste you back" is the local phrase for "Do come again soon." "What about some 'you and me'?" asks the East-End Londoner, "you and me" being Cockney rhyming slang for "tea." "Good-evening, together," says the resident of Norwich when we might say, "Good evening, all of you." "Now don't fash yourself," says the Dorset farmer, meaning, "Don't go to any trouble." Even the names of English towns are pronounced differently by people in different places. People who live in Shrewsbury call the town "Shrowsbury"; outsiders invariably pronounce the name as it looks.

Americans traveling in Britain wonder why so many ways of speaking English continue to be used. Habit and pride in the home locality are probably the chief reasons nowadays, but until recently there were others as well. Travel was difficult and expensive until railroads came into use only a little more than a hundred years ago, and farming folk rarely heard anything different from the local speech. In the hills, where roads were not much better than rough tracks and where the isolated inhabitants continued to do their daily work exactly as it had been done for centuries, there was no need to find or invent new words or phrases. But in Lowland Britain, the speech of each district changed as foreigners settled down and began to work among the local people. The Danes who conquered a large portion of England in the ninth century, the Flemings who came to live in the eastern counties, the French Huguenots who fled to England in the seventeenth century all left their mark on the speech as well as on the customs and the character of the populations of which they became a part.

And so even the flat districts of Lowland Britain have an interest of their own, apart from the literary and historical associations that cling to places scattered all over the country. The green Midland county of Warwickshire would have been worth visiting, even if Shakespeare had not come from there, because Warwickshire speech, Warwickshire folklore, Warwickshire customs all have their special flavor. Similarly, Americans visiting East Anglia because many of the early American colonists came from this area, might start with historical interests but would soon find themselves fascinated by the countryside and the ways of the people who live there.

East Anglia is not a name usually found on a map although it is much used in daily conversation. Once upon a time there were seven kingdoms in England and some of the names of these ancient kingdoms have never been forgotten. For instance, the Kingdom of the West Saxons was called Wessex, and the word "Wessex" is still used to refer to a large area that includes the chalk plateau of

Hampshire that we visited in our last chapter, and also Wiltshire, Gloucester, Dorset and Somerset. In the same way, East Anglia was once the Kingdom of the Eastern Angles, and includes most of the county of Essex directly east of London, the two counties of Norfolk and Suffolk (the North Folk and the South Folk) and Cambridgeshire.

In ancient and medieval times East Anglia was almost an island. The sea bounded it on the east and the north, and southward from the inlet called the Wash lay an area of swamps over which no roads could be built. People coming to East Anglia had to follow a ridge which ran into the area from the southwest. Even in Roman times, two thousand years ago, the road that ran along this ridge was an old one; it is still called the Icknield Way after the tribe of ancient Britons whose kingdom this was.

Control of that single precious road was of great importance in time of war, and so the Romans built a garrison town which we call Colchester to guard the southern end of the highway. Colchester is still a garrison town, though the soldiers who are stationed there today look very different from the legionnaires who marched along the little streets up the steep hill to the castle which the Romans built, with their thin red bricks laid slantwise in a herringbone pattern. The castle is still there, and boys and girls from schools in neighboring towns come to see it and to look at the Roman necklaces and the rings, the glass vases, the water jugs, the tools and the coins that have been found in the ground when streets were repaired or wells dug or walls torn down.

North of Colchester there are no more hills of any size. Instead, for mile after mile there are some of the finest farms in England. The soil is deep and fertile and has the benefit of winter frosts which do not affect land in the Southwest. There is just enough rain to please the farmers, and far more sunshine than most areas receive in Britain.

In the Middle Ages all of the eastern counties raised wool, and the harbors along the east coast—Ipswich, Aldeburgh, Southwold,

Yarmouth—were full of sailing vessels which carried the wool across the North Sea to be spun and woven in the mills of Belgium. As time went on, the East Anglians decided to learn to spin and weave their own wool. Farmers' wives and daughters spun the yarn; every farmhouse had a loom or two and traveling weavers came around to make the "English cloth" which was sold over much of the civilized world. So wealthy did these hard-working farmer-manu-facturers become that in every East Anglian village they built a huge and very beautiful parish church to the glory of God, and these noble churches in the Gothic architecture of the fourteenth and fifteenth centuries still tower majestically over the hamlets into which those prosperous wool-working villages have declined.

When machinery was invented and it became possible to manu-facture cloth on a very much bigger scale than ever before, in factories operated on power derived from coal, East Anglia lost its wool trade. The eastern counties were too far from the coal-fields, and the wool merchants in Yorkshire gained an immediate ad-vantage over their once-prosperous rivals. However, the East Ang-lians still had their good soil, and before long they worked out such an excellent system of crop rotation—wheat, root crops, barley or oats and clover or beans—that farmers in other parts of the country followed their example and England became a grain-exporting country in the early 1700's. Since that time East Anglia has never lost her position as one of the leading agricultural areas in the country, even though hundreds of acres of her best flat farmland were used for air bases both by the R.A.F. and by the American Eighth Air Force during the war.

Unlike any other section of England is the portion of East Anglia known as the Fens, or the Parts of Holland. The Fens are the great swamps that lie to the south of the Wash. These swamps have an exciting history of their own. Centuries ago low islands rose here and there just a few feet above the level of the swamp, and on these islands lived hermits, political refugees from the outside world, swamp-men who made a living both off the water and the land.

The largest island of all was called the Isle of Ely, and there monks built a great cathedral.

Just as it is still unwise for people who do not know their way about to wander through the swamps of Georgia for fear of getting lost, so it was unwise for any outsider to try to investigate the mysteries of the old Fens. Not only was he likely to get lost; the swamp-men did not like company and they took care to discourage any curiosity on the part of the outsiders. Tax-collectors could whistle for their taxes, King's messengers could cry their messages in vain. In time of war their swamps were a last place of safety in which a hard-pushed army of Fenmen could gather their resources. As a result, Fenmen never admitted defeat.

But time—and hard work—have changed the Fens. The early Britons and the Romans drained small areas of land. Then, in 1630, the first large-scale project was undertaken. A land-owner called the Earl of Bedford formed a company of "adventurers" to drain the Fens around the Isle of Ely in the same way in which the Dutch had succeeded in draining their lowland areas. A Dutch engineer advised the company to dig a canal seventy feet wide and twenty-one miles long to catch the water which until then had spread through the marshes. Twenty years later another canal was dug, parallel to the first, and very soon the land that had been drained in that manner was being turned to pasture and plow-land of the richest kind.

Meanwhile, the stilt-walking swamp-men, who suddenly saw their occupations gone as fishing, basket-making, bird-catching and other swamp activities became impossible, grew very angry and for years waged bitter war against the drainage workers. When the water had been drained much of the land shrank below sea level, as it had in Holland, and dykes like the Dutch dykes had to be built to keep the sea from flowing over the fields. Then pumps, some-times powered by windmills as in Holland, had to be installed on the dykes, to lift the water into the drainage canals, which were now higher than the fields themselves. The Fenmen cut the dykes as fast as they were built and added seriously both to the cost and the time required to carry out the great drainage scheme.

Nevertheless, the work went on, and when the Earl of Bedford's first project proved successful, other sections of the swamp were drained as well. Altogether a region roughly eighty miles long by thirty miles wide has been added to the area of England, and now only one or two small patches of original Fenland are left undrained. Some of the pumps that are in use have been operating day and night for more than a hundred years; others are just being installed. Wheat, oats, potatoes, sugar beet, mustard, fruit, bulbs and flowers are raised on a commercial scale in the Fenland area.

Very different from the East Anglian lowlands are the Midland shires or counties, which form a triangle with York just inside the northern angle, Bristol marking the southwestern one and the Wash making the third. The Midland counties are surrounded by hills —the Pennines on the north, the Welsh mountains on the west, and a belt of hills called the Scarplands running from the south to the east coast of Lincolnshire and Yorkshire. This is the heart of England. Largely agricultural, with each county seat built on a river so that farmers could bring their produce to market, the Midlands now contain much of the recent industrial development of Britain as well, and the region around Birmingham has had an increase in population second only to that in the London area.

Although most of the Midlands consist of a grassy plain, here and there in this rolling sea of fertile farmland is an island of rock and coal. One of these coal-fields supplies fuel to Coventry; another to nearby Birmingham. Factories stand near Sherwood Forest, where Robin Hood once roamed in Nottinghamshire. The old local industries have acquired national importance. Once the cobblers of Leicester made shoes by hand out of leather bought from farmers who slaughtered their own cattle for meat to be salted down for the winter; now Leicester manufactures and distributes not only a fair proportion of all the shoes worn in Britain, but is a manufacturing center for shoe-making machinery upon which other shoe-making towns such as Northampton and Kettering depend.

But although times have changed, there are still many reminders of the past in the old market towns. In Shrewsbury there are fine half-timbered houses that were old in Queen Elizabeth's time; in Rothwell, there is a market house that was built in 1577; a dozen places have fine town halls. Sixteenth-century and twentieth-century buildings elbow each other along the town "high" streets. It is this mixture of old things and new, both in familiar daily use, that gives England some of its special character. That mixture of old and new is as rich in the industrial cities of the Midlands as it is anywhere in the country.

CHAPTER FOUR

Highland Britain

WEST and north of the line from the Tees to the Exe lies Highland Britain. Generally speaking, life in the hills is hard. But the struggle against Nature has produced tough breeds of men, and the Highland people have influenced British life far more than their numbers would suggest. The main area of Highland Britain is Scotland, whose beauty and history require a book to themselves. When the Scots say, "We're like the red deer; only a bullet will stop us," they mean it. Germans and Japanese who fought against Scottish regiments, known as "The Ladies from Hell" because they wore kilts as part of their dress uniform, agree that often one bullet was not enough.

But in addition to Scotland, Highland Britain includes three very important districts south of the Border. These are the peninsulas which jut out from the western side of England—Cornwall, Wales and the Lake District of Cumberland. These are the lands of the legends—the lands of Cornish King Arthur, his knights of the Round Table and his fabulous city of Camelot, of the Welsh bards, and farther north, of the lords of the Border who acknowledged no sovereign but ruled their domains and fought their wars in their own bold way.

The counties of Devon and Cornwall are England's little California, though you do not have to be a Californian to realize that the comparison can be pushed too far. However, it is surprising that any comparison can be made at all between the two regions, since these southernmost counties of England lie much farther north than any part of California. They are in the same latitude as British Columbia. Their annual range of temperature is the narrowest in Britain; in fact, in Cornwall there is scarcely any difference between the summer and winter. Cornish children rarely see snow; neither do they swim off sun-scorched beaches whose sands burn the soles of their bare feet. Swimming can be delightful on the Cornish and Devon coasts but most Americans will sunbathe only, in the sheltered nooks among the great crags, or in the tiny golden coves where the cool breezes cannot find them.

Not everyone would like to live in a climate in which the temperature remains almost constantly in the 50's. But to the market gardeners and flower growers of Cornwall and Devon the mildness of the winter gives many advantages. Here as in California and Florida are grown fruits, vegetables and flowers for winter and spring markets which other sections of the country cannot supply. Wildflowers abound where the soil is too thin and poor for cultivation. In February the hillsides are carpeted with pale yellow primroses for anyone to gather and send to the London flower-stalls. Only a little later there are acres of daffodils, both wild and cultivated; then acres of tulips heading the whole royal procession of garden flowers from lupines and roses to gladiolus and roses to chrysanthemums and roses again.

But Cornwall and Devon have a history and character more rugged than descriptions of their lush green landscapes suggest. Cornwall's coast is stern, with high gray cliffs looming grimly over tiny harbors once haunted by fierce smugglers and by the "Wreckers" who cruelly set up lights to lead sailing ships on to destruction on the rocks so that they could loot them later. Bold men, too, were the fishermen who sailed out of the harbors of Padstow, St. Ives, Falmouth, Fowey and Mevagissey, and who in times past waged bitter war against their racial cousins and rivals, the Breton fishermen from France. But in 1940, when France fell, the Bretons knew well that they could find a friendly refuge in the little ports of Cornwall, and hundreds of fishing craft slipped across the heavily mined waters of the Channel.

The Cornish people are Celts, like the Bretons, Welsh and Irish, and like them, they once spoke Gaelic rather than English. Some claim a slight mixture of Spanish blood as well, brought in by survivors of the great Spanish Armada which was wrecked when it tried to invade England in 1588. Nevertheless, the people of Cornwall are a less mixed race than "the English" (a Cornishman does not really consider himself English any more than a Welshman does). In the days when there were few roads, and all of them bad, Cornwall was too far away from London to attract much attention from the king or other outsiders. Except for the Celts themselves, who drove the earlier inhabitants out of Cornwall and Wales as early as four thousand five hundred years ago, no invaders succeeded in completely subduing these counties, and they were left untouched by the culture of the Romans, the Anglo-Saxons, the Danes and the Normans long after each of these had affected life in other parts of the country. It is not surprising that legend places King Arthur's stronghold at Tintagel, where a ruined castle stands high on the cliff jutting out over the sea, for King Arthur is thought to have been in real life a great leader of the Celts (or Cornishmen) against the invading Anglo-Saxons.

Under the rolling plateau surface of Cornwall is some of the oldest rock in Britain but the surface soil is generally richer than in other Highlands. There are no mountains, but here and there in the midst of a large patch of poor soil left to the sheep and the wild ponies there rises a noble hill. Such are the hills known as Brown Willy, and Rough (pronounced to rhyme with "bough") Tor, which stand a thousand feet above the surrounding Bodmin Moor.

And what is a moor? The words "moor" and "heath" are both used in reference to open wasteland with only a few clumps of trees but covered with the wiry shrub called heather and a prickly shrub called gorse. A heath is usually flat, a moor hilly. Both are green all year round except in August, when the flowering of the heather wraps them in purple, a sight worth traveling far to see.

Some of the stretches of Montana desert look like the moors except for the differences in color.

The wealth of words in the English language describing types of landscape gives delight to the language expert but is often a handicap to the ordinary American reader. Just as the British have difficulty with American terms like "bluff," "mesa" or "prairie" we often read descriptions of English scenes without being sure we completely understand them. In Britain each district has its own names for things. For instance, a deep narrow ravine running to the sea is called a coomb in Cornwall and Devon, a chine in Hampshire and the Isle of Wight, a dale in Yorkshire, and a glen in Scotland. But although a Scotch glen and a Devon coomb can look very much alike, they are never exactly the same—some of the flowers that grow in Devon do not grow in Scotland, the trees are not the same, the rock is of a different color.

Cornwall, Devon and Somerset are commonly called "the West Country" but Devon and Somerset are much less wild than Cornwall, and their history has always been closely bound up with that of the rest of England. While Cornwall remained Celtic, Devon and Somerset were colonized first by the Saxons and then by the Normans, who became the Saxons' overlords. For four hundred years Devon and west Somerset folk made their living chiefly out of wool and the shipment of it overseas. When the development of factories requiring fuel killed much of the trade of East Anglia, it also killed the wool industry of the West Country. Devon, Cornwall and Somerset had no cheap sources of power. Their harbors were too small for steamships, and tin-mining both in Cornwall and Devon had become too expensive to be profitable. For a while life was cruelly hard in the beautiful western valleys, and in the picturesque and once-prosperous villages family after family pulled up stakes and set out for the American colonies or Canada, or, later, Australia or New Zealand.

Better fortune has returned with the automobile, which has brought in an enormous tourist trade, and with fast transportation which makes it possible for West Country farmers to sell their finest and most perishable products far afield. We Americans may have our strawberry-shortcake, for instance; in England, people prefer strawberries with Devonshire clotted cream—the thickest of thick golden cream slowly cooked on the back of the farmhouse range. Both dishes are so good that it is as well that they are national, not international favorites, and you rarely have to choose between them.

Other industries, too, have either recovered some of their past importance or have recently sprung up to supply new demands. For instance, there are the tin mines, some of which are thought to date from before the Roman invasion in 55 B.C. By 1922, although plenty of ore remained, most of the mines were so deep and required so much pumping to keep the lower levels dry that mining costs were extremely high. Besides, some miners were old-fashioned and did not want to start using newer methods which might have kept the costs down, particularly where newer methods would require fewer workers. So Malayan tin was brought in, instead, and the West Country miners lost their jobs altogether. Since then the pendulum has swung. Malayan tin began to get expensive, and when the threat and then the outbreak of war jeopardized shipping, the tin, and also arsenic, tungsten and wolfram deposits in Cornwall and Devon became very important. Some of the old mines in the Redruth and Camborne district are in full operation again. Others are being pumped out and restored.

Cornwall and Devon are also sources of kaolin or china clay, which is used to add weight and finish to paper and cotton materials as well as to make chinaware.

Devon's capital is the beautiful cathedral city of Exeter, but Americans take special interest in Plymouth, the port from which the Pilgrims sailed in *The Mayflower* on September 6th, 1620, on their voyage to the New World.

Exmoor in Devon is the scene of a romantic story which millions of young people have loved, Blackmore's *Lorna Doone*.

To travel northwestward from Devon into Wales is to leave England and to enter a new and strange country. It is small, perhaps, and thinly populated, but it has a beauty that is entirely its own, a language of its own, a history and a culture of its own. In the rugged mountains of North Wales the villages lie miles apart and there are few passers-by to greet the sheep-farmer as he mends the old stone walls that run steeply up the mountainside and along the narrow road. In the winter, rain and mist float through the green valleys, although the peaks of old Snowdon and the hills around are capped with snow. In the summer the sun shines impartially on the climbers making their slow careful way over the rocks to the refreshment hut on Snowdon's summit, and on the swimmers splashing energetically in the blue waters of the Irish Sea, with Harlech's old gray castle looking down on them from its hill above their golden bay.

Every coal-mining community in America has its quota of men from South Wales, the tough patient men of laughter who dug the great coal mines in the steep valleys of their homeland. South Wales consists almost entirely of a high plateau covering the coal-beds, so the mines have been built in the ravines cut by rivers, and the tiny gray stone houses of the miners, with their black slate roofs, line the roads and paths that run sharply up the sides of the valley. Here railroads were in use before steam engines. Coal was loaded on wagons at the head of the ravine, a railed track was built down toward the mouth of the valley, and the wagons ran down along the rails all by themselves. To enjoy the lovely colors of the moors and the great expanse of open sky, which cannot be seen from the dark village, people often climb a steep footpath from the top of the town up to the edge of the plateau.

Even in times of prosperity the lay-out of a Welsh mining town was not conducive to high spirits. But worse was to come. Steamships began to burn oil rather than fine hard coal for fuel and Wales lost her coal markets. Year after year men were unemployed because their mines were closed and no other industry settled in the gray villages. Some miners joined the unemployed in London. Many Welsh people have unusually beautiful voices and groups of jobless miners sang their old Welsh songs on the city streets and then passed the hat to obtain pennies to rent beds for the night. Their families lived on their unemployment insurance (known as the "dole" in England). Even now, behind whatever labor troubles break out in the prosperous Wales of the 1960's, where there is much new industry, there lie the memory and the fear of unemployment.

More than the English or the Americans, the Welsh people honor their poets, musicians and orators. For hundreds and hundreds of years every Welsh village has had its annual competition to select its own contestants to send to the national "Eisteddfod," and the honor of being chaired as the bard or of winning a crown is as highly prized as, in America, election to an All-American football team. For all that, the Welsh are no mean athletes.

All that they do, the Welsh do whole-heartedly. Strong Methodists, like the Cornish, they astonish less fervent Puritans by the strictness of their observance of Sundays. Trains and buses stop running; men, women and children wear their best black hats and coats, black stockings, shoes and gloves and stroll sedately to chapel whence their magnificent singing can be heard down the valley; all laughter and idle chatter is frowned upon, and only hymns may be played or sung in the evening when the family gathers around the massive upright piano. And yet on week-days there are none so merry as the Welsh.

In England, as in the United States, Northerners and Southerners differ in outlook and in customs. To know the English it is not enough to know the wise-cracking Cockneys of London; you must also meet the Liverpuddlians of Liverpool and the Mancunians of Manchester, a city which boasts that "What Manchester thinks today England will think tomorrow." Londoners may disagree, but there are ultra-modern model towns, factories and schools in Yorkshire and Lancashire that put the South to shame. However, development is patchy and some of the northern towns are notoriously dirty and ugly.

The life of England depends to a very great extent on both the farming and the industry of the North. Northern England is both highland and lowland. The highlands include the mountainous and very beautiful Lake District and the range of the Pennine Hills which runs, with intersecting gaps, southward from the Scottish Border down to a famous hill called The Peak in the center of England. The main lowland area of the North is the Lancashire plain, which extends forty or fifty miles inland from the Irish Sea to the Pennines, and which is linked with the Midland plain. Here food is raised to feed the people who work in the cotton factories of a dozen Lancashire cities, in the soap works and chemical industries near Liverpool, in the glass works at St. Helens, in the coal mines, in the silk mills and in the potteries.

East of the Pennines are the wild Yorkshire moors, which Emily Brontë described in *Wuthering Heights*. The three divisions of the county of Yorkshire are called Ridings, the word being an old one meaning a third. Since Yorkshire cannot have four thirds, there is no South Riding at all, only the North, East and West. The West Riding contains wool manufacturing towns which a hundred and fifty years ago won the trade from their East Anglian and Devonshire rivals because Yorkshire had, in the sides of the Pennines, plenty of coal for her new factories.

One of the loveliest cities in England is York, with its thirteen-hundred-year-old cathedral, its ancient stone city walls, and it memories of the Roman legions who once tramped the streets when York was Eboracum and the Romans were building the great wall that still stretches across the north of England from the Solway Firth to the Tyne River. In those days the Picts who lived in Scotland were fierce warriors and bad neighbors, and for centuries to come the Border saw a good deal of fighting one way or another. Now everything is peaceful, but the old walls and castles are permanent memorials to a fighting past, and the North never forgets it has fighting blood in its veins.

CHAPTER FIVE

Home Life in Britain

THE house stands in the middle of a row of identical red brick houses, all joined together, all facing a row similar in every respect, except that halfway down the street there is a gap where two or three were bombed in 1940. It is a modern house, as they go in England—forty years old, perhaps. It is built well, with large bay windows, a shiny black front door with a polished brass knocker, high-ceilinged rooms and an air of spaciousness inside that you do not expect to find after looking at the rather narrow façade. It is the sort of house that millions of people in England call "home."

It was built at a time when making arrangements to avoid extra work laid a person open to the charge of being lazy rather than clever. It has a long unheated scullery or sink-room extending into the back garden, and an old-fashioned kitchen containing a coal stove for heating water, a gas stove for cooking, a plastic-topped table, a kitchen cabinet, an open china cupboard and a couple of painted armchairs. One of these is usually occupied by the family's black cat—black cats are considered lucky in England.

At the front of the house is the sitting-room, with its easy chairs drawn up in front of the tiled fireplace in which a coal fire burns on winter afternoons and evenings. There is a folding gate-leg table in the bay window, an upright piano with candlesticks on each side of the music rack, in one corner of the room. In a recess beside the fireplace sits a table holding a television set. White net curtains hang at the windows, with artificial silk drapes at each side ready to be drawn together at dusk.

Halfway up the stairs is a landing off which opens a large green and yellow bathroom containing a six-foot-long bathtub with fancy curved legs, a big white hand basin, and a linen cupboard built around the hot water pipes. The rest of the plumbing is in a little room next door.

There are two bedrooms, a large and a small one, on each of the second and third floors. Bedroom fireplaces in which coal was once burned now contain gas or electric heaters but heat in a bedroom is regarded as an expensive luxury and the British usually use hotwater bottles or electric pads to warm the beds in their chilly rooms. Each bedroom also holds a wardrobe cupboard since the only closet in the house is the slant-ceilinged one under the stairs, which the family used as an air raid shelter during the war.

With thirty-two steps to climb, with coal fires to build and replenish daily, with the kitchen sink fifteen feet distant from the kitchen stove and the dining table at the other end of the house, it is not an easy home for a woman to take care of. But until Mrs. Smith, who lives there, had to do war work in addition to housework, she was not really aware of its defects. Until 1939 she considered keeping house a full-time job and was content that it should be so. It was true that sweeping ashes out of the fireplace made a lot of dust each morning and that carrying a scuttle of coal to the third floor was hard work, but the family enjoyed watching the flames of the open fire as they sat in the parlor listening to the radio in the evening, and the children did not have to have a fire every night. Stairs were stairs, but she did not mind them.

After all, when the children were little, Mr. and Mrs. Smith had often taken them, each in a seat slung from the handlebars, a full thirty miles on a day's outing by bicycle. Those days were almost forgotten after the family acquired a midget automobile, but when the war deprived civilians of gasoline for their cars, the bicycles proved as useful and even as enjoyable as ever. Granny Jones, Mrs. Smith's sixty-two-year-old mother, who lived a mile or two away, dug out her bicycle as well, and pedaled back and forth cheerfully on her way to peel vegetables at the soldiers' canteen.

Mrs. Smith knew perfectly well that her life in England was in some ways harder than that of many women in the United States. Years ago, her younger sister had gone to Providence, Rhode Island, as secretary to an American businessman, and had later married there. When she came back in the Coronation year of 1937 to visit her family, she described her own labor-saving kitchen, the laundry room in her basement, the open archways possible in a completely heated house. Mrs. Smith listened with interest and conceded that owning a washing machine might make washing "smalls" for the children easier, though she would still prefer to send the sheets and towels to the laundry to save the nuisance of having to dry them in England's showery climate. The other things she considered more suitable to America than to England. She could see no point in operating a refrigerator in the winter when the airy larder or pantry was cold enough to keep food sweet; besides it struck her as being absurd to uphold the delights of ice-cream desserts all year round if, like Gertrude, you were constantly fearful of gaining weight and hardly dared eat a full meal, ice cream or no ice cream. Mrs. Smith was sure that not having an open fireplace in a room would make the air stuffy whenever the windows were closed, and although her sister Gertrude's brightly painted kitchen equipment sounded very attractive, it was years before she thought of painting her own cozy, comfortable—and shabby—furniture.

Although Gertrude considered her sister woefully old-fashioned as a housewife, she whole-heartedly admired her skill as a mother. The Smith children, tall, fair-haired and red-cheeked, were as beautiful as angels, and though their behavior did not always come up to their appearance, their American aunt found them quieter in manner and more courteous than her own beloved but nerve-wrackingly noisy brood. Discipline both at home and in school appeared to be very much stricter than in America. The wishes of the children themselves were less frequently consulted and their opinions on matters concerning the family as a whole were less seriously considered than in her own home, and yet everyone seemed content with whatever arrangements were made.

All of the children, including nine-year-old Nancy and six-year-old Timothy, had small allowances, but none had ever earned a penny. By this time, Dennis, aged fourteen, would long since have had his turn at selling papers in America. As for twelve-year-old Janey, she was shocked to hear that girls in the United States accepted payment for the neighborly act of taking care of someone's baby; that seemed to her to be wrong.

Generally speaking, although much of the work the older children did in school was approximately two years in advance of that done by people of their own age in the United States, their aunt felt that her English nieces and nephews had had far less social experience than her own children had at home.

In 1937, however, she could not foresee that one of the effects of the war on the children would be to hasten their development, in a year or two making them more mature, though they remained less sophisticated, in the popular sense of the word, than their American cousins. The Smiths lived outside a large city, in an area officially classified "safe," and the children were not, therefore, evacuated to more remote districts like the hundreds of thousands of city children, who had suddenly to be picked up and dropped into new and strange homes, to be cared for by strangers. Nor were they quite far enough away from the center of the city to have evacuees assigned to them, although Mrs. Smith was told that in an emergency she must be prepared to take in two children or a mother with a very small baby.

But even without the strain of going into an unfamiliar home or of having strangers in their own, the young Smiths had to get used to all sorts of new conditions. For one thing, soon after Dunkirk, their father went into the army. Then came the raids of the next autumn, when, safe area or no, stray planes flew overhead and occasionally jettisoned their bombs as they fled from a pursuing Spitfire. Timothy and Nancy learned to hide their fear lest they upset each other, while Dennis and Janey began to keep a watchful eye on their extremely worried mother. When the "All Clear" blew at four or five in the morning, it was always Janey who, stiff and tired, nonetheless scrambled to her feet with, "Look, mummy, I'll make you a cup of tea," while Dennis carried the sleeping young ones upstairs to their beds. When the bombs fell on the houses down the street, bringing down the top floor ceilings of the Smith house, shattering windows, and blanketing the whole inside of the house with plaster dust and soot, it was Janey who promptly took the two youngsters to Granny's and then came back to help her mother do a housecleaning that made an ordinary spring-cleaning seem light by comparison. Meanwhile, Dennis unearthed some old linoleum and nailed it across the gaping windows to keep out the rain and cold until the repair squads came with some glass five or six months later.

Aunt Gertrude in 1937 could foresee none of that. But even before the war had tested the stamina of her young relatives, she liked much of what she saw of them and of their life at home. Although the relationship between parents and children was never described as one in which all were "pals" together, there was no doubt that English children and their parents enjoyed each other and played together with zest. In the harsh years to come Aunt Gertrude often found herself remembering Janey's thirteenth birthday party, for instance.

Janey had chosen her guests without the slightest concern over their ages. They included seventy-five-year-old Mrs. Loomis, young Mr. and Mrs. Edwards, and three-year-old Gregory Mason, who was not much good at games, it is true, but who was carried home to bed early in the evening anyway, so that it did not matter. Before that dreadful catastrophe occurred both Gregory and his hostess had a wonderful time. Then, of course, there were Granny and Aunt Gertrude and Uncle Phil, who had been in the last war and was deaf, and various Smith cousins. And finally there were Janey's best friends from school.

It was a very gay party. First they all played paper and pencil guessing games together. Then they had what Janey called a "wizard spread": sandwiches and cheese sticks and potato chips and ginger beer, with chocolate eclairs and ice cream to follow. And there were paper hats, and snapping crackers to pull, with a prize for every single person instead of just one for the person who gets the right number.

After that the youngest guests were carried off to bed, and the rest began to play charades. There was a false start when Janey decreed that the groups should act out the names of heroines of English history and everyone thought simultaneously of Florence Nightingale and began to plan the scenes for "night," "in" and "gale." When Mrs. Smith, who was busy providing old curtains and out-of-date clothes for costumes, realized what was happening, "Nightingale" was banned. Later there was an international incident when Aunt Gertrude objected strenuously to having Pocahontas classified as a heroine of English history; she was strictly American, said Aunt Gertrude. But majority opinion was against her. Pocahontas had saved the life of an Englishman, had married another Englishman, had come to make her home in England and was buried not far from London. So the Pocahontas charade was accepted.

But though Janey's birthday party was fun, it was a very small affair by comparison with a coming-of-age party. An English twenty-first birthday party is like all the American graduation parties rolled into one. The best of clothes, of flowers, of music, and of catering are provided to honor the event.

Aunt Gertrude often wished that the best of catering were provided a little more frequently in England. English cooking at its best was undoubtedly very good. The roast beef of old England deserves its fame. English sea-foods—fat scallops, tiny oysters, delicate Dover sole, pungent kippered herring—are as good to dream of as America's shad and roe or brook trout or salmon cheeks. Coming home to tea in front of the open fire, with scones that melted in your mouth and the thick hot pancakes called "crumpets" oozing with butter and honey, was a foreshadowing of heaven it-self. But, thought Aunt Gertrude wryly, the soggy boiled potatoes and cabbage and boiled mutton of popular restaurants fore-shadowed just the opposite, and the average meal, however well cooked, lacked variety. English taste forbids the combination of hot and cold or sweet and salty dishes; consequently meals includ-ing hot food rarely include a salad, and a true-blue Englishman finds it difficult to believe that anyone can really like so strange a combination as waffles with syrup and pork sausages.

Not that British taste approves the insipid. Many English people enjoy the strongest of curries and condiments. Furthermore, the dampness of the climate makes the use of salt-shakers impractical because the salt sticks in the holes, and so most people in England dip each morsel of food into a pile of salt on their plates, thus taking three times as much as the average foreigner. But each to his taste is a slogan befitting civilized mankind, and if Aunt Ger-trude found herself slightly wistful, like all Americans, over the apparent British incapacity to make good American coffee, she knew that when she got back home to the States she would be equally wistful, like all the British, over the apparent American incapacity to make good English tea.

Except, perhaps, with regard to food, Aunt Gertrude found in her former countrymen a curious intertwining of sentiment and pure realism, of common sense and whimsy. An Englishman sees nothing odd about calling his small brick bungalow "Mt. Everest" because he is fond of mountain scenery, though anything less like Mt. Everest could hardly be imagined. That is sentiment. On the other hand, he thought it entirely reasonable to celebrate King George VI's birthday in June, despite the fact that the King was born in December. After all a celebration demands good weather and England rarely has good weather in December. That is realism. Londoners line up quietly for rush-hour buses and get home more quickly and less exhausted than New Yorkers who push and scram-ble. That is common sense. But, following the tradition handed down from stage-coach days, the English route their buses from one "public house" to another, and the already bewildered stranger finds that he must remember to take a 91 bus at a "pub" called "The Hand and Flower," change to a 7 at "The Packhorse and Talbot," whatever that means, and finally get off at "The Crooked Billet." It is clear from names such as these that the license to keep an English pub includes a certain amount of poetic license as well.

The English pub is something more than an inn; it is a national institution which allows adults to enjoy the company of others for as little or as long as they like, without becoming involved in a formal organization like a club. Not that there are no clubs in England; on the contrary, men's, women's and young people's organizations are very active indeed. Many of them, including Rotary Clubs, Y.M.C.A. and Y.W.C.A. groups, women's clubs and Scouts, have international connections. But the local pub is the place where the men congregate of an evening to drink a glass of beer, to discuss politics, to philosophize, and to play shove-ha'penny and darts. Television, which has proved too strong a competitor for many movie theaters, has had much less effect, although clearly it has had some, on pubs.

That the pub is far more than a place at which food and drink are sold was proved repeatedly during the war when pub-keepers were obliged by law to keep their premises open even when they had nothing at all to sell. In the past it has often been the village pub which has carried on the education of the local citizens where the schools too soon left off. Men who on one evening discuss why a cage containing a bird on a perch weighs more than a cage containing a bird on the wing, and on the next, debate the gold standard, acquire both independence of thought and a flexibility of mind that attendance at schools and movies and lectures often fails to develop.

Whether, indeed, most English schools try to develop either independence of thought or flexibility of mind as such is doubtful. What they try to develop is simply the mind, and to that purpose they expect their students to work harder than Americans, though not so hard as the schools of some Continental countries. Before 1947, free education was provided for all children between the ages of five and fourteen and children who passed scholarship examinations were eligible for further free education at grammar schools giving pre-university courses. Most "public" schools also admitted a number of scholarship students and more than half the students attending universities, including Oxford and Cambridge, received scholarships of one kind or another. But many children who won scholarships did not accept them because their families needed the wages they could earn at work. So, although it was possible for a boy or girl of any social background to attend excellent schools and universities and to receive a superb education, the total number who did so was small and the majority of children in the country left school at fourteen.

This system was obviously not good enough for a modern nation. In 1944 a new law was passed raising the school-leaving age to fifteen by 1947 and promising (a promise still unkept) to raise it to sixteen as soon as more teachers, textbooks and space in schools could be provided. It also attempted to make the best use of the insufficient educational facilities of the country by setting up an examination system designed to send children at the age of eleven into the sort of school for which they were best suited. All children in state schools had to take this so-called eleven-plus exam, and of these approximately a fifth were admitted to grammar schools for pre-university courses. The others were sent to secondary modern or technical schools offering many (and often excellent) vocational courses but no advanced science, mathematics or languages—subjects required for university entrance. Although some attempt was made to provide for late developers and occasional changing of courses, by and large this meant that a child's entire future depended on the result of an examination taken when he was eleven years old.

Many of the results of this system were unforeseen. It had been hoped that no-one would feel a sense of failure if he was not chosen for grammar school education; in practice many children suffered deeply and some had nervous breakdowns. On the whole, grammar schools functioned well but some of the other schools, with their mass of children who felt rejected, had discipline problems of a kind hitherto unknown in England. In the comparatively small number of high schools of the American type, where all kinds of courses were offered to a student body much larger than that of the average English school of, say, two hundred children, and where the grammar school stream was only one of many, there were fewer problems of adjustment. But these schools were built only as an experiment and it took time to prove their worth.

The eleven-plus system is still used in England but local education authorities have met the wide-spread dissatisfaction with it in various ways. Some refuse to use the exam itself but choose children for grammar schools on some other basis. Still others have added science, languages and mathematics to their secondary modern school courses though there is a serious shortage of teachers of these subjects. More comprehensive high schools are also being built.

At higher levels of education, existing universities have been enlarged and new ones established, while technical institutes have been vastly improved and modernized.

All in all, much has been done to improve education generally without lowering the standard so long provided for brilliant students. But no-one is satisfied with what has been achieved. Britain needs a very high quality of education because, not having great natural resources, she has to earn her living by her "know-how."

CHAPTER SIX

Farming in Britain

AMERICAN soldiers who, while they were stationed in English villages during the war, used to visit the local schools and talk to the children there about life in the United States, were sometimes taken aback when they were asked, "How big is an American farm?" Later they realized that some of the youngsters expected all farms in the United States to be very large because the country is so large. Similarly, the American soldiers themselves were rather surprised when they learned that some farms in England comprise several thousand acres; they had thought that because the country is small all its farms were likely to be small.

Of course, farmers in both countries know that the size of a farm ought to depend on what kind of farm it is. Nowadays most farms in England are dairy farms and the great majority of them have less than a hundred acres. The most profitable farms in England are those between a hundred and a hundred and fifty acres in size. However, in some counties half the farms have less than fifty acres.

The tenant of a fifty-acre farm in England does not get rich but often he and his family are very happy as they are. Most of the fifty-acre farmers do not even own their farms, since much of the land in England is owned by great land-owners who will lease a farm to a man or his heirs for as long as ninety-nine years, but will not sell it outright. Often the same family has leased a farm for centuries, buying a new lease each time the old one comes to an end. This system of selling leases rather than the land itself is one reason why the British have generally favored government ownership of land more than Americans do. So long as the government buys the land and pays for it fairly, so that no injustice is done to the private owners, the average person would rather see the rent go thereafter to the government for the benefit of the country as a whole than to the handful of fortunate families who own miles but have refused to sell any part of it outright to the men who actually work on it.

But the important thing about farming is not who owns the land but what comes out of it. For thousands of years what came out of it varied only with the soil and the climate. The Egyptians, the Greeks, the Romans, the British of Chaucer's time all had roughly the same scanty knowledge of farming methods and used equally crude tools—plows that only scratched the surface of the earth, flails to beat out the grain from the straw at harvest time. Most countries had the same sort of system of village agriculture: the pasture belonged to everyone and each farmer had the right to feed a cow and a pig or two off it, but the plowed land was divided into strips owned or rented by each farmer separately. Each farmer lived in the village, rather than alone on his own land, and going back and forth to work and from one strip to another took up a good deal of time in itself.

As long as farming was carried on under this ancient system, there was never any extra food and in periods of bad weather many people starved because they had no reserves of grain to fall back on. But it was not easy to change the system because people were afraid that when the common pastures were cut up they might not get enough land to support their cattle, or that when the strips of plowed land were joined together so that a man's farm was all in one place rather than scattered around the village, they might not receive as good a piece of land as they had had before. So the old system continued in some countries until less than a hundred years ago.

In England, the change began very early—in the 1300's. While, little by little, the population of the country increased, the folk on the land (and they included the bulk of the population) managed to produce just enough food to feed everyone most of the time, and enough wool, not only to clothe the country but to sell abroad in ever greater quantities. When the Flemish weavers moved from Holland to East Anglia to teach the English farmers their wool-craft, they also taught them their love of gardening, and people began to raise vegetables. The ships that carried wool across the sea brought new kinds of food home with them—potatoes from America, for instance.

So new ideas were brought to England, and farmers began to think that perhaps the old ways were not always the best. They began to try out new plans for themselves. They started to rotate their crops so that the soil would not be starved; they decided to pen their sheep in a new place every night, fencing them with movable hurdles, so that the sheep manure would fertilize the pasture and prepare it for the plow. They began to give the cattle extra food in the winter instead of killing them off in the fall or leaving them to get what nourishment they could out of the thin winter grass. New tools came into use, and with them new methods of making hay, of using silage, of draining the soil. With better food, cattle and sheep grew larger; with more food, human beings grew larger too, until now neither the average American nor English-man can squeeze himself into the suit of armor worn by a medieval knight. England began to sell grain to other countries; at home even the poorest people in the land stopped eating the wholesome but coarse brown bread which was the food of all the peasants of Europe and demanded the white wheat bread that had once been reserved for the rich.

That was two hundred years ago. When machines were invented and factories sprang into existence, England changed very quickly from a farming country into a manufacturing country. Many of the farmers went to work in the factories and instead of producing her own food, England began to buy her wheat from the United States and Canada, her meat from Argentina and Australia, her butter and eggs from Denmark, Norway and Holland. Many farmers wanted very much to stay on the land but they could not lower the cost of their farming enough to meet the competition of large-scale farming in newly settled countries, and particularly in the wheat belt of the United States. When World War II began in 1939, English farms were going to seed while two-thirds of the country's food came in from overseas.

Within a few weeks, England faced a serious risk of starvation, as ships that had previously brought in food now had to be loaded with troops or munitions, and others still carrying grain or meat fell victims to the U-boats. It was the farmers who saved the country —the farmers, their families and the girls who joined the Land Army, and to a lesser extent, the evacuees from towns who learned how to "lift" sugar beets, and the vacationers who spent their vacations making hay or digging potatoes. The farmers decided that they could double the amount of food that Britain had produced even though they had fewer men on the job, and they did it.

Tommy Heston's letters to his cousin Jack give you an idea of how the miracle was accomplished. Tommy's father owns fifty acres and rents an adjoining eighty in Shropshire, a pleasant agricultural county lying between the Welsh mountains and the Midland plain. In 1941 Tommy was fifteen and hoping to have a year at Reading University, like Jack, studying scientific dairy farming, before going into the Army. While Jack was shifted from an anti-aircraft base in the South of England to another in the Orkneys and from the Orkneys to North Africa, Tommy's letters followed with their account of a farmer's family at war.

Hoary Underhill
Anesley
Salop
2nd February, 1941

DEAR JACK,

Have you shot down any JU 88's yet? Or have the blighters decided you're too hot for them and begun to avoid your corner of

England? Rabbit-shooting will seem awfully dull after all this, won't it.

You will be surprised to hear I weigh over eleven stone *—eleven stone five, to be exact. Mother says it's extraordinary how I've suddenly stopped being a big boy and have turned into a big man. I tell you this by way of warning so you won't have a heart-attack when you come home on leave, and also by way of explanation. I can't get a leather jacket like yours to wear in this raw weather, and you said yours was tight for you across the shoulders. So I've been wearing it; fire a shot or two in my direction if you mind and I will give it back. I don't know whether it's having the village full of evacuees or whether stocks are low everywhere, but it's getting harder and harder to find clothes to buy.

Father's been put on the War Agricultural Executive Committee and spends all his time at meetings. The Committee has set production quotas for all the farms in the county, and now everyone's working like mad trying to reach them. The smaller farmers say it's hopeless but Father says they just don't want to change their ways until they are sure the new ones will work. It's all very complicated because they are trying to increase milk production and at the same time they are plowing up some of the pastures for wheat. Bill and I have started to keep a milk yield record for every cow.

All the best,
TOMMY

17th April, 1941

DEAR JACK,

Haven't you got some leave coming soon? Underhill has two new inhabitants—no, I'm not talking about the animals, though they've increased in number too. Father's taken two Land Army girls, real Cockneys from London, and what good they'll be he says he doesn't know, but being on the W.A.E.C. he has to make this farm an ex-

* One stone = 14 lbs.

ample and he had to get somebody. They aren't completely green; Doreen, the one that used to be a manicurist, is wonderful at milking.

Father's been asked to experiment with plowing; he's been using a W.A.E.C. tractor to pull a two-furrow plow in one field and a three-furrow one in another, and comparing running costs. So far the three-furrow plowing takes less time and does not cost more. When they have worked out the best way of setting the plow, particularly on the hilly fields, they will ask all the farmers to use the same system.

We're gradually cutting down on the number of chickens we keep. We can't get the food for them because so much of it used to be imported.

The wheat we sowed in the autumn is coming up very nicely. Father says there's a proverb that it ought to cover a hare in March and it would have. But why should a hare be covered with wheat anyway? Do you know?

I forgot to say Doreen is a blonde. She says she used to have red fingernails like the girls in the colored adverts in American magazines. She says she used to dress ever so smartly before the war. I'm sure she'd think you were ever so nice. It's ever so restful here —would be ever such a nice change for you. Meanwhile, give Jerry one for me.

All the best,
Tommy

August 9th, 1941

Dear Jack,

I meant to drop you a line the moment school broke up for the summer holiday, but the farm has kept us all busy. Father's very bucked about the way the W.A.E.C.'s plans are working out. We got the hay in on every farm in the area despite the very broken weather. The crops on what used to be pastures are better than we could have hoped for, though it's true the land was naturally well fertilized. The new pastures are good too, and we are getting four gallons a day from our best milch cows. Ley farming is going to be the thing, with everyone taking the plow around the farm; what the farmers here are arguing about is whether the pastures ought to be turned over to crops at five or seven year intervals or longer, and how often they ought to be plowed and fresh grass seed sown.

I think I forgot to tell you we plowed up the cricket ground in the village so that the London evacuees could "dig for victory."

I almost forgot to ask you to answer a question to settle an argument between Bill and Doreen. He says that in the Orkneys you can see the midnight sun. She says no because her brother was in the Orkneys and that was not very far from Scotland. So I said maybe you can see the midnight sun in the north of Scotland. Can you?

All the best,

TOMMY

12th November, 1941

DEAR JACK,

We have formed a Young Farmers' Club in the village and I was elected president. The organizer came down from the Ministry of Agriculture and told us about 4-H Clubs in America, and about Young Farmers' Clubs here, and we are planning a pig-raising contest and learning about judging cattle, and we are going to have a Christmas party in the village hall.

Mr. Gregory, who owns the big estate east of us, told Father he considers £1-0-0 per acre per year a reasonable profit for a farmer. Father was very annoyed about it; he says it's all right for men with several thousand acres to be content with £1-0-0 from each, but a man with fifty or a hundred acres has to do a good deal better than that if he's going to support his family.

The Young Farmers' leader was saying that in America they sometimes have sunny weather for a solid two or three weeks at harvest time and can get it all done at once. Poor us—we think we're lucky if we have two sunny days together, and it takes us from August to November to get the crops in at all. But he says that in a year or two our production per acre will be the highest in the world if we all work at it.

Laugh if you want—Father is asking to have another Land Army girl assigned to Underhill. Now that he's got used to Doreen and Mabel he thinks they're wonderful.

Mummy wants to know if you've had all her letters and the cigarettes we send each week. How long does it take for a letter to reach you in Africa?

I meant to ask you if you have ever seen a grass-drying machine —the sort that makes better winter feed for cattle than hay or silage? Father says a few have been in use for years but they are too expensive for ordinary farmers to buy. Maybe after the war we can keep the Agricultural Committees and let them buy expensive equipment, the way they have done during the war, so that all the farmers in an area could use it by turn. They say Britain is already the most highly mechanized farming country in the world, but I don't believe it. Maybe we will be when we can get the machines after the war. Meanwhile, I'm sure someone in the United States has invented a weeding machine that does away with all old-fashioned kneeling and bending. What do you think?

Believe it or not, I have thirty lines of Latin to do tonight, this evening, right soon as the Yanks would say—or would they? I'm always at sea with Yank slang.

All the best,

TOMMY

CHAPTER SEVEN

England's Wealth and Resources

IT WAS a fine autumn evening fifteen years after the end of World War II and the train that went speeding through the East Anglian farmlands seemed strange to the tall American ex-sergeant who had come back to take a look at places he had known in the war. Many of the men who had been here with him would, like him, have stared incredulously at the half-empty compartments; for the rest of their lives they would remember standing in the corridors of English trains, straddling baggage and making jokes or singing in the blackout. England without the crowding and the blackout would hardly have seemed England.

But now in 1960 there was no blackout and no crowd. The American looked out at the farms with their clumps of trees, golden, brown and russet, but rarely crimson like the maples in New Hampshire. The hedges were still green except for runaway patches of red Virginia creeper. In the gathering dusk the gardens that lined the railroad track in the towns were full of pale roses, asters, dahlias and chrysanthemums. Lights began to shine through unshaded windows.

The ex-GI pulled out a package of cigarettes and offered it to the middle-aged man in the blue suit sitting opposite him.

"Last time I came this way England still had the blackout," he said. "Nice to see the lights." The Englishman laid his paper aside, glad to talk once more with one of the Yanks whose behavior had puzzled, delighted, amused and impressed him during the past years.

"Yes, quite," he said smiling in agreement. "I don't think anyone who lived through the war years ever takes lights entirely for granted or forgets what it was like to creep in and fumble around during the blackout before you could turn a light on. I suppose you got as used to all that as we did. How long were you over here?"

"Two years. I was a sergeant when I left."

"Like England?"

"Sure I like it, on the whole. I've been wanting to see it looking normal in peace-time. It's a pretty country and I get along with the people. But I tell you honestly, there are lots of things I don't understand about this country."

"Well, there's usually a reason for everything. What sort of thing don't you understand?"

"Of course I have to admit things have changed since the war. There are more cars now and the stores are full of stuff. But many people still don't have cars or labor-saving devices and wages are still low. And things are so small—tiny little cars, tiny freight-cars, tiny washing-machines. And some things are old-fashioned."

The Englishman laughed.

"Well, Sergeant, you've covered a lot of territory in those few remarks, and a lot of us would agree with you on some points. We are getting cars—too many for our roads—and we've got labor-saving devices for our homes but most of us still do not have the luxury equipment you Americans all have. Our standard of living is the highest in Europe, I believe, but it must seem low compared with yours. Have you ever thought why it is lower?"

"Well, people don't seem to want—" the American began.

"Nonsense," said the Englishman. "We'd like to have most of the things you've got—even big cars if we had room for them—and certainly more refrigerators and washing-machines and central heating if we could afford them. So far they've been expensive. It's true we have more sales resistance, as I think you Yanks call it, than your people, and in some ways it may be a bad thing. But the difference in the standard of living is not simply the result of a difference in the temperament of the people. Think of the difference in our national resources."

"The United States has practically all the minerals it needs, I guess, and plenty of oil and quite a lot of wood, though I admit we wasted a lot of what we used to have."

"I don't know about that. The important point is that you are still one of the richest countries in the world in raw materials. You have, as you say, plentiful supplies of iron, silver, copper, tin, coal, oil, and, for that matter, food. Your population runs about fifty people to the mile, on the average. Your wealth divided among fifty people to the mile is bound to make each person richer than our very, very much smaller resources divided among approximately eight hundred people per mile. We have a great deal of coal, particularly in the North and in South Wales, and it is located close to our own iron ore and close enough to the sea for convenient shipping. But coal is one of the few things we do have enough of. By careful conservation and replanting, we get a little wood out of our forests, but when you consider that we have been using them for two thousand years you can see why our supplies can only take care of part of the demand for pit props, furniture, wooden implements and so on; wood pulp for paper has to come from outside. We have small quantities of other minerals besides coal, and good supplies of china clay. Considering that farmers are only about 6 percent of our population, the land is very productive. Our home-grown wool remains the finest in the world; I suppose you've seen the big woolen shawls that are light and warm and yet so fine that they can be pulled through a ring off your finger? That just shows you. You know we get around forty bushels of wheat to the acre. And I think we may do better in the future. But even if we do I don't think we'll have even a moderately good diet if we have to depend on our own resources for all our food. We'll be short of butter and cheese and meat and bread, to say nothing of fruit most of the year. Of course we have good supplies of fish, and that helps. But we have to divide the wealth from the resources we do have among about seven hundred and ninety people per square mile."

"My gosh," said the American, "I never thought of it that way. I always figured it was because you were slow and old-fashioned that you didn't have as much modern equipment as we have. Now you've got me wondering how in the world you make as decent a life for your people as you do. Even if you haven't as much as we have, you certainly are not badly off and I'll say this for you: you never see folks here living in the shacks some of our folks used to live in back home. I don't see how, if you have so little to spread among so many, you each get so much. Or is it that you make your money out of the wealth of your colonies, like Canada and India?"

"Don't let Canadians or Indians hear you call their countries colonies," said the Englishman with a smile. "They are completely independent—as independent as you Yanks! So are Malaya, Ghana, Pakistan—and there are others. But we don't get any profit in the way of taxes even from the colonies that we still administer; sometimes we tax ourselves to help them. Our government gets no revenue from outside at all. However, you are right in thinking that some of our income must be brought in. Much of it comes from foreign trade, and that is why foreign trade is necessary to us."

The American leaned forward in his seat.

"There it is again—foreign trade. I keep hearing about foreign trade. Maybe I'm dumb but I just don't get it. Buy and sell—sure, I understand all that. I can see why you have to buy a lot of things—part of your food, all your oil and gasoline, most of your wood and iron and aluminum and gold. But what are you going to sell? You haven't got a thing. Well, a little coal and wool, but what else?"

"Our work," said the Englishman.

"What do you mean, your work?"

"Just that," said the Englishman. "We've got a lot of people crowded into this little island. They are our wealth. The more people we've got, the more brains, the more skill, the more technical knowledge, the more experience, the more muscle we've got to the square mile. We can bring in supplies of iron ore, let our people get to work on it, supplying their skill and experience, and turn out high-grade machine tools. We can import raw cotton and turn out top-quality cotton prints. We can sell the finished products for more than we paid for the raw materials, and the profit we have earned by our labor and skill will help make up for our poverty in supplies. That seems fair to you, doesn't it?"

"I suppose so," said the American. "The only thing is that we and other nations want to do the same thing and I don't see where you are going to fit in. How can you import raw materials from all over the world and compete with us? Your stuff must be expensive."

"Maybe so, though we can haul things halfway round the world by sea as cheaply as you can haul them across your country by land. But if our products are good enough it won't matter if they are a little more expensive than others. We hope that we shall be able to make them good enough. We have a great store of craftsmanship in this country, a tradition of skill handed down from the time before mass production came in. We are fairly inventive: before the war we led the world in television, and during the war we developed radar, the Bailey bridge, the Mulberry harbor, the jet-propelled airplane—well, you know the list. I have the very greatest admiration for you Americans, not only for your inventiveness but for your magnificent way of rushing things through. But I think you will agree that you have no monopoly of ability."

"I still think you're up against a tough proposition. We make high-quality goods too. We're not going to buy them from you. We've got to keep our own people employed. Heck, we might be having a recession and a lot of people out of work. I'm scared every time we have a little slump. The way I see it, we've got to sell, not buy."

"Right," said the Englishman. "If that's the way it is, that's the way it is. You can't buy from us; therefore we can't buy from you. Our pound notes are only pieces of paper so far as you're concerned. If we can't pay you for what we buy, in dollars which you have paid us for what you bought here, we can't pay you and that means we can't buy from you. Trade is a two- or a four- or a ten- or a twenty-way business but it never goes one way only."

"Okay," said the American. "Let's skip it. I'll think that over later. Let's get back to where we started. I still think you're pretty old-fashioned, and you haven't persuaded me that I'm wrong."

"Well, now," the Englishman grinned, "I'm not even going to try. In the line of machinery, of equipment for our factories and homes, we often are old-fashioned. Sometimes it's true that we just don't want to change things. Often it's for a better reason than that."

"I can't see a good reason for being old-fashioned. It seems dumb."

"It would be even more stupid to throw away something we can't replace. Another thing is that with smaller resources we can't afford to be as wasteful as you Americans. But I think that really to understand why we hang on to things you have to know something of our history. You know there was a time, not so long ago, when England was called the workshop of the world. Doubtless sooner or later someone else would have done it if we had not, but we really invented the modern factory system. We got a head start on everyone else and became a rich nation as a result, but we have had to pay for our success. Let's suppose that my great-grandfather built the first pipe and tube factory in the world. He designed the machinery, laid out the floor plan, assigned jobs to his workmen. It cost a lot of money but he put in the best equipment he could get. When the factory was built he turned out excellent pipes and tubes which were sold all over England. As time went on, he noticed a number of ways in which his original plan might be improved, but it would have cost a lot to rip up the machines and plan a new lay-out, so he continued as before. Ten years after he started, one of his workmen went to America and started a similar pipe factory in New York, putting in the improvements which my great-grandfather felt he could not afford to make. But in his turn, the workman noticed that there were other possibilities of improvement, and when he set up a new plant to take care of the business that was growing in the Middle West, he built the finest model factory of all. Later a rival firm started in California, with a still more economical plant, and to meet their competition the original American manufacturer brought the two earlier factories up to date. In a young expanding country it was bound to pay."

The ex-GI nodded.

"And meanwhile your great-gran'daddy went on running his old factory in the same old way."

"Exactly. He had to watch his expenditure because he did not have the growing market you Americans had. So he let his plant get more and more out of date, until finally he could not see how he could ever afford to modernize it. That's the way it has been in our coal industry and our cotton mills. Mind you, we have our modern plants too, and even during the war our productivity increased by 15 percent. Some of our problems are of our own making—I know that. Our workers, for instance, resent changes in methods and relations between worker and boss are too much influenced by memories of past troubles. But our biggest need is to modernize our industry."

"So you still go on using these little freight cars and tiny automobiles because you have not been able to modernize the factories that produce them?"

"No, Sergeant, that's a different story altogether. Not everything unlike your products is out-of-date or inefficient. In this country it's more efficient to use the smaller goods wagons and cars. If we used large freight cars, as you call them, we should have to ship them from one place to another half empty, or else fill them up but take them on a roundabout route to leave their goods at various destinations. But a small car can be filled up and shipped from one point to another directly and cheaply. As for automobiles, our needs are again rather different from yours. We don't ask for cars in which to make two-thousand-mile journeys over the Rockies and through your American desert. We rarely drive more than two or three hundred miles. But since our petrol and oil are imported, they are expensive and we want a maximum of mileage per gallon."

"Yes, I can see that your needs often must be different from ours. But what about your low wages, or is that explained by there being so much less to go around than we have in the States?"

Big Ben clock tower and Abraham Lincoln statue in Parliament Square, London

The White Cliffs on the south coast of England

Magdalen Tower looks down on Oxford High Street

Daffodil time in Regent's Park, London

Market Square in Dunster, Somerset

Hawthorn hedges fence the fields of Southern England

English housewives chat over the flower garden fence

A thatcher at work on a half-timbered Tudor cottage in Herefordshire

British Official Photo

British Official Photo

The chalk hills called the South Downs, in Sussex

Prehistoric Stonehenge on Salisbury Plain

British Official Photo

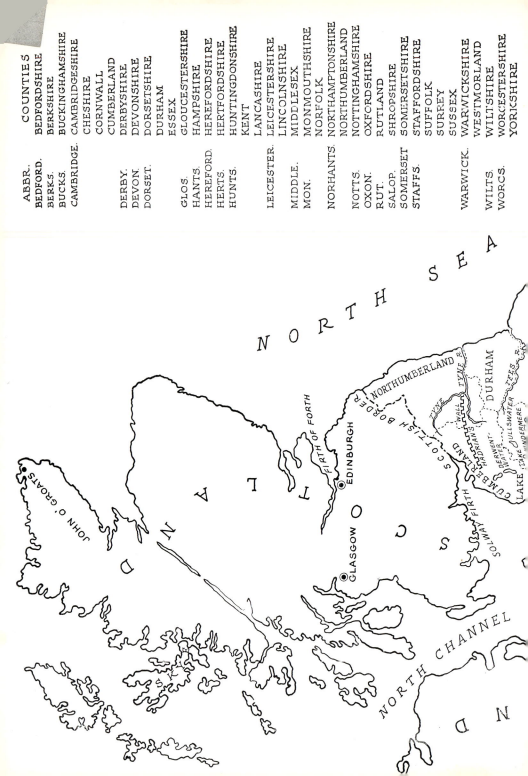

COUNTIES

ABBR.	
	BEDFORDSHIRE
BEDFORD.	BERKSHIRE
BERKS.	BUCKINGHAMSHIRE
BUCKS.	CAMBRIDGESHIRE
CAMBRIDGE.	CHESHIRE
	CORNWALL
	CUMBERLAND
DERBY.	DERBYSHIRE
DEVON.	DEVONSHIRE
DORSET.	DORSETSHIRE
	DURHAM
	ESSEX
GLOS.	GLOUCESTERSHIRE
HANTS.	HAMPSHIRE
HEREFORD.	HEREFORDSHIRE
HERTS.	HERTFORDSHIRE
HUNTS.	HUNTINGDONSHIRE
	KENT
	LANCASHIRE
LEICESTER.	LEICESTERSHIRE
	LINCOLNSHIRE
MIDDLE.	MIDDLESEX
MON.	MONMOUTHSHIRE
	NORFOLK
NORHANTS.	NORTHAMPTONSHIRE
	NORTHUMBERLAND
NOTTS.	NOTTINGHAMSHIRE
OXON.	OXFORDSHIRE
RUT.	RUTLAND
SALOP.	SHROPSHIRE
SOMERSET	SOMERSETSHIRE
STAFFS.	STAFFORDSHIRE
	SUFFOLK
	SURREY
	SUSSEX
WARWICK.	WARWICKSHIRE
	WESTMORLAND
WILTS.	WILTSHIRE
WORCS.	WORCESTERSHIRE
	YORKSHIRE

NORTH SEA

NORTH

FIRTH OF FORTH

NORTHUMBERLAND

TYNE R.

DURHAM

S C O T L A N D

JOHN O'GROATS

⊙ EDINBURGH

SCOTTISH BORDER

TYNE
WALL
HADRIAN'S
DERWENT
WATER

TEES R.

ULLSWATER
LAKE WINDERMERE

CUMBERLAND

LAKE

⊙ GLASGOW

SOLWAY FIRTH

NORTH CHANNEL

N D

Southampton Docks are visited by vessels from every corner of the world

Fishermen haul in the herring nets in the English Channel

A postman on duty on the Yorkshire Moors

The Roman city walls and the Minster towers at York

The flat country of the Fens in East Anglia

The lofty lantern tower of Ely Cathedral can be seen for miles across the Fens

The prehistoric earthwork of "King Arthur's Castle"
at Tintagel on the Cornish coast

The harbor of the Cornish fishing village of Polperro

On the top of **Hey Tor**, Dartmoor, Devon

The coast and mountains of North Wales

A coal mining village in Wales

"I think it is, partly. But other things come into it too: for instance, the older machinery in use in some factories makes it impossible for us to equal the amount your workmen produce in a modern plant, and the climate (particularly the lack of sunshine) makes it harder for anyone working in this country to put so much drive into a day's work. But there is another very important point. We can afford to work for lower wages because our rents are lower than yours and we have more services provided by the State than you do in many sections of your country."

"Now you're touching politics, Sir, and that's a big subject in itself. It looks as if we're pulling into London so there won't be time to discuss that tonight, I guess. All the same, I wish I could figure out what is happening politically in this country. I was in England for two years and I still don't understand where Queen Elizabeth fits in, and Parliament, and all the rest of it."

"Have you read anything about the history of this country?"

"Not much."

"Well," said the Englishman, getting up to take his bag down from the rack as the train slowed to a stop in the big London station, "I've been feeling ashamed for some time because I know so little about your American history. I'll make a bargain with you. I'll get hold of a book about it and learn as much as I can about your people if you do the same about us. If you do, I think you'll find that what is happening in England today is a continuation of tendencies that began to develop centuries ago. We'll both understand each other better if we find out what made us the sort of countries we are. What do you say?"

"I'll shake on it, Sir," said the American. "It's been very interesting meeting you."

"And for me, meeting you. I wish you all the best. Well, as you Yanks say—so long!"

The American grinned.

"Cheerio," said he.

CHAPTER EIGHT

How England Became English
2500 B.C.—A.D. 1066

WHEN English boys and girls groan over their books of English history it is usually because there is so much of it. By comparison, the study of American history, with a straightforward account of the War of Independence, the settling of the Middle and Far West, and the Civil War seems wonderfully simple. Schoolmasters who have been struggling to fit in all the kings from Arthur who fought the Saxons, and Alfred who fought the Danes, to George VI who fought the Nazis, find thirty-three presidents easy to remember and six weeks of American history during the summer term a pleasant introduction to the August vacation.

And yet students in England do have one advantage over students in more recently developed countries like our own. They can see the marks of their history all around them. Of course even in a young country like the United States we are surrounded by signs of the past although we do not always recognize them. We write "1 lb. of apples" just as people do in England, without stopping to think that lb. is the Latin abbreviation for "pound" handed down to us from the days when people who could read and write always used Latin. We see a nun without noticing that she wears the kind of clothes all ladies wore in the Middle Ages. In our early settlements, old churches and missions and museums, our imagination finds a door to the past. But it is a door that many of us cannot open very often because we live too far away from these things.

In England, on the other hand, just as you cannot go far from the sea, you cannot escape the sense of the past. Heroes of real life or of story have trodden every footpath; every village has known a king; great men are buried in every churchyard. Until 1940 wars left England almost untouched; even now in the open country the "cottages" of the common people and the castles of the great alike withstand centuries of use and weather. The churches have blocked up an old window here or built a new tower there, but they list their clergy in an unbroken line from the twelfth century to the twentieth. Many an unimportant English village can point to itself unmistakably labeled, though oddly spelled, on a map drawn to help the knights setting off on the Crusades to the Holy Land six hundred years ago. The high-school students in Missoula, Montana (founded in 1861) were probably amused when, in exchange for a scrapbook they had made about their home town, they received one from a school in Ilkley, Yorkshire, with an essay in it stating that "The modern history of Ilkley began in A.D. 600." But that sentence was written in all seriousness by boys and girls who felt just such a sense of kinship with their ancestors of that long-gone epoch as we all feel toward the founders of our home towns. All that lies between A.D. 600 and the middle of the twentieth century lives in their memories as a magnificent pageant in which they themselves will also have a rôle.

Nevertheless the choice of a date as early as 600 to mark the beginning of modern history is unusual even in England, where 1485 is the date suggested in most textbooks as the most convenient dividing line between the Middle Ages and the modern period. In actual fact there was no break at that time with what was already a long and colorful past. There is no written record of the very earliest part of English history. All that we know about it we have learned from burial mounds and from the weapons, tools and dishes which archeologists have dug up near the sites of ancient earthworks. Man is said to have appeared in what is now England approximately 550,000 years ago, and there are many signs that Britain has been inhabited since the Stone Age. At that time the British Isles were still joined to the Continent by a land bridge, and people from the

Mediterranean regions were able to move westward unhindered by water. Farmers of the southwest of England must often think of those early ancestors of theirs, for as they cultivate their fields they often have to guide their plows around a huge granite boulder, or a group of two or three granite boulders standing on end and rising ten or fifteen feet above the ground. These stones were set up approximately four thousand years ago, when they figured in the religious ceremonies of the Brythons, the folk from whom Britain was to take her name. The religious capital of these West Country people was at a place called Stonehenge, where a great circle of granite slabs bears witness even now to their piety and their skill as engineers. How these dark little men mustered enough power to drag for miles and to hoist into place slabs weighing tens of tons no one really knows.

Centuries went by while the tribes of Britain planted their crops and dug in their tin mines and married and bore children and died in the little villages strung out along the ridges of the downs and the plateaus overlooking the heavily forested and swampy lowlands. Then, in 55 B.C., Julius Cæsar and his Romans crossed the Channel from France in their first invasion of the island from which their Gallic enemies had received supplies and reinforcements. On August 11, 1945, while the world waited breathlessly for news of the surrender of the Japanese and the end of World War II, the British Broadcasting Corporation devoted its Children's Hour program to a celebration of the 2,000th anniversary of that early trans-Channel invasion which changed for all time the map of England and the language and the culture of all English-speaking people. Thousands of the soldiers who had crossed the Channel in the other direction in June, 1944 had read about Cæsar's invasion in their school Latin classes. But there was no time, as they were tossed about in their landing craft to remember the Roman legions in *their* invasion barges, or as the Allied troops saw their Mulberry harbor battered and broken by gales, to recall the storm that wrecked Cæsar's fleet and forced an early "strategic withdrawal" from the Kentish coast. Yet those Roman invaders and the armed forces of the United Nations rode those stormy waters in obedience to the same truth—that no power can hold Europe west of the Rhine unless he has mastery of Britain and the English Channel.

Cæsar's second invasion was more successful than the first, for he defeated the British chief Cassivellaunus before he led his army back again to Gaul. The Roman legions did not return, however, until A.D. 43, nearly ninety years later. Then they stayed, and for the next four hundred years almost the whole of England was governed by the Romans. From city to city and camp to strongpoint the roads were laid, over which legions of soldiers could be moved rapidly in times of trouble. They were narrow roads but paved with such huge blocks of stone that the road bed is firm two thousand years later, and they run straight across whatever hills or swamps lie in their path, from Londinium to Camulodunum, which later became Colchester; from Londinium north to Eboracum (York) and beyond, to the wall that Hadrian built; from Londinium to Uriconium (Shrewsbury) to Mancunium (Manchester); from Londinium to Durnovaria, that became Dorchester, and Regnum, that became Portsmouth, and east to Dubræ or Dover. By their spiderweb of roads centering on London the Romans made London the capital of England.

In the far north, Hadrian's Wall, built in A.D. 123, and the wall of Antoninus, built in A.D. 140, kept out the barbarians of unconquered Scotland. In Wales and Cornwall the Britons were able to cling to their ancient customs and lead their own lives unobserved by sandaled centurions from Italy. Elsewhere, the Roman temples to Jupiter, Mars and Minerva rose on sites which Christians later seized for their churches—St. Paul's hill in London, for instance. Roman villas with mosaic floors and colonnaded terraces dotted the countryside; Roman baths and hot-air furnaces provided their inhabitants with a degree of comfort scarcely to be equaled in the average British home of the early twentieth century. In the open-air theatres Romanized Britons watched the Roman games. Roman troops set the pattern for all invaders to come by marrying native girls, and the legions that held the country in the fifth century were largely recruited from local men.

Most important of all was the fact that when Rome became Christian, Britain too was converted. Later, new invasions of barbarians from the east and north destroyed many traces of that early Christian church in Britain, but in Ireland and the Western Isles the flame of faith continued to burn until a new wave of missionaries came to reconvert the pagans of Anglo-Saxon England.

For the rule of Rome came suddenly to an end. Down from the north swept the Goths to threaten Rome itself. All Europe was in turmoil; the legions and the fleet that Rome had sent to guard the southeastern coast of England, the "Saxon Shore," were called back home to defend the Capital of the Empire. As late as the year 446 Roman Britain was begging for help, but begging in vain. The storm broke. The Celts from Ireland invaded England from the west; the barbarians from Scotland invaded from the north; the Saxons from Germany invaded from the east. Many of the Britons in Cornwall crossed the Channel and settled in what we call Brittany, in France. Others simply withdrew to their own hiding-places in the hills, leaving their homesteads to the Saxons, many of whom stopped fighting and settled down as farmers as soon as they found land that pleased them.

It was a time of change, but what was happening at one place might have no effect at all on something quite different that was happening fifty miles away. While Christian missionaries were building monasteries in Wales, the Cornish King Arthur was fighting a last desperate war with a handful of men against the Saxon invaders. Almost nothing is known about that real King Arthur except that he was so brave a man and so beloved a leader that when at last he was killed the story of his deeds became a legend embroidered by generations of poets. It was only in their tale that the little Cornish market town of Camelford became the tall-towered "Camelot"; that Merlin, the magician, lifted the infant Arthur from the crest of the sea's ninth wave, and the fifth-century tribesmen became the polished knights of medieval chivalry.

For roughly a hundred years, from A.D. 450 to 550, the Angles and Saxons from northwest Germany and some Jutes from the lower Rhine invaded and colonized Britain. Members of the defeated British tribes became serfs; the strongest of the Saxon sea-chiefs became kings, though their territory was often no larger than a single modern county. As time went on, British settlements and Saxon towns existed side by side, each people learning from the other. The Saxons were rude rough men, highly practical, full of vigor, and above all, men of the sea. The British were more civilized and very artistic, but were moody and less persistent than their conquerors. Each needed something of the other's character, and each received it, particularly after Augustine came to convert the pagans and the whole island became Christian.

For two hundred years and more Britain was free from invasion, and the Romano-British-Saxon population produced some of the greatest men of the time. But in 850 invasions came again, this time from Norway and Denmark. Once again a vigorous sea-faring folk sailed down the rivers and swarmed over the lands of the peace-loving farmers. Once again the sea-farers won. East Anglia, Essex, half of the Midlands fell to the Danes. Even London was theirs, although across the river Thames lay unconquered Wessex. Had it not been for one man, England might today be a Scandinavian country.

The man who kept England English was King Alfred, ruler of the kingdom of the West Saxons. Defeated on land, driven to hiding in the forests and seeking shelter among his own peasants, Alfred decided that he must defeat the Danes at sea. He built the first British navy, and won his battle to keep Wessex safe, although he could not dislodge the Danes from the "Danelaw" which they had already conquered. For a thousand years after King Alfred's time the British have remembered the lesson he taught them, the lesson that Britain must defend herself at sea.

CHAPTER NINE

The Middle Ages
1066—1485

THE map of England, like the map of the United States, is studded with names of a strange and delightful variety. There are towns with names of Celtic origin—*Marazion, Penryn, Polperro* in Cornwall; *Dolgelly, Aberystwith, Llandudno, Criccieth* and hundreds more in Wales; and *London* and *Coventry* in other parts of the country. There are the names of the Roman garrison towns with the word castra (camp) transformed into chester—*Chester* itself, *Winchester, Cirencester, Dorchester* or *Leicester*. There are the Anglo-Saxon names, *Chipping, Kensington, Twyford, Isleworth, Nether Wallop, Shepton Mallet, Melksham;* and the Danish names, *Halvergate, Skegness, Holmfirth*. And here and there among them all is a name that looks half English, half French—*Ashby de la Zouche, Thorpe le Soken, Turville, Belvoir*. These French names are only a small part of the heritage of the Norman Conquest of England, the last of the great invasions that left their mark on the character of the population, the laws, the language, customs and culture of England.

On the south coast, some fifty miles from London, lies the town of Hastings. A few miles north of Hastings there is a ridge called Senlac, and it was here that in the year 1066 William the Conqueror won the throne, not of Wessex only but of all of England. For since the time of King Alfred of Wessex and the rule of the Danes in the Danelaw, England had been unified, first by a victory of the Saxons and then by a later victory of the Danes under King Canute. When Edward the Confessor, the last king of Alfred's line died, three men claimed the throne: Harold, son of Godwin, who was immediately crowned, Harold Hardrada of the Danish line, and William of Normandy. William was King Edward's cousin and he claimed that Harold, son of Godwin, had once taken an oath promising fidelity to him and giving up the throne of England. Be that as it may, the newly crowned King Harold was attacked, first by Harold Hardrada and immediately after the latter's defeat, by William of Normandy.

During World War II, when the boys and old men of England spent their evenings and week-ends training themselves as members of the Home Guard to defend England if the Germans came, many of them thought with a new understanding about the men in that Home Guard which tried to defend England against the Norman invader. The Saxons called their defense unit a "fyrd" but it was a "home guard" all the same—"a multitude of home-spun folk" Brett Young calls it—as poorly equipped with weapons as the patrols who faced the German hosts in 1940 with one rifle shared among six men. King Harold had a bodyguard of three thousand trained soldiers highly skilled in the use of the Nordic battle-axe, and a larger body of well-equipped freemen, but many of his more humble followers came carrying pitchforks for want of better weapons. William had five thousand mounted knights, trained in the newer methods of warfare, the use of the lance and the sword.

Men on both sides fought bravely. Down a thousand years of history has come the story of William's brave minstrel, Taillefer, who rode out ahead of all the Norman cavalry, tossing his sword in the air and catching it as he galloped forward singing a song of battle until at last the Saxon axes caught him and hewed him down. So, too, has come the story of King Harold's courage, though all the odds were against him and in the end he was slain by a Norman arrow. William of Normandy became King of England. England and France had been joined together in a curious bond of friendship and enmity which was to continue through centuries.

From the point of view of the defeated English, the Norman victory was a heart-breaking tragedy. William's followers had come in order to enrich themselves, and their reward for fighting consisted of lands which William took away from their Saxon owners.

But the Normans brought with them much that was good and that would in the long run be helpful to England. Everywhere people were tired of change, of constant movements of population as invasions came first from one quarter and then from another.

Things were in a muddle. And then suddenly the Normans were there, laying down definite and clearcut rules, organizing the life of the Church, regulating the activities of every member of society.

The Normans introduced into England the feudal system, under which the lords of the manor owed allegiance to the king, from whom they held their lands, and were in turn owed allegiance by their tenants. The tenants, both freemen and serfs, were bound to the land; that is, they were not allowed to move away from their farms and work elsewhere. Serfs had to work for the lord of the manor a certain number of days a year without payment. On the other hand, they could not be fired or turned out of their homes by the lord and he owed them his protection and care in times of danger. In England, feudalism was never quite so rigid a type of society as it was in France, because even under the Normans many of the laws of the native English were retained and allowed members of the lower classes more freedom than they might have had otherwise. That is why there was room even under feudalism for the steady growth of personal liberty.

How much the British prized their personal liberty in those days is clearly shown in their reaction to the survey for the Domesday Book. Soon after William the Conqueror had been crowned in Westminster Abbey he gave orders that a complete record should be compiled of all the property in his English realm, farms, houses, cattle, with the value of each and the names of their last two owners. Two copies of Domesday Book still exist. There is no record like it in any other country in the world, for so complete is the information given that a farmer cultivating his land in the 1960's can find out from the Domesday Book which parts of his farm were used as pasture, which were plowed and which were still wooded back in the year 1086. All the same, though the British are glad to have the Domesday Book now, they objected strongly to the survey when it was first made, feeling that the king ought to have been ashamed to pry into people's personal affairs.

Like the Romans, the Normans were excellent engineers and builders. Instead of small, dark, round or barnlike churches such as the Saxons had built, the Normans built or planned the construction of many of the great cathedrals which rank among the most beautiful buildings in the world. In Canterbury Cathedral, in the Tower of London, in dozens of other places we can see the round Norman arches with their zigzag decorations, the sturdy columns that for eight hundred years have borne the weight of the high-arched roof.

One after the other, the Normans solved the problems they met as they tried to build out of whatever materials lay close at hand, whether it was granite, small stone or rubble or even Roman brick from some deserted Roman temple or theatre. Little by little they learned to build pointed arches instead of round ones, to put two or three or five little arched windows together instead of spacing them widely apart. Sometimes it took a very long time to build a church and while it was being built the workmen developed new ideas about the way in which they wanted it done. So in one thick stone wall we see the single round windows of the early builders; in another, the same sort of windows grouped in threes, while to the east there is a great window with the slender pointed arches that are no longer Norman, but Gothic, architecture. If it were not true that until the middle of the nineteenth century the builders —masons, bricklayers, stone-carvers and carpenters—of England understood the rules of good proportion better than some highly trained architects do today, the results of their work would not only have been hideous but their buildings would have crumbled into ruin long ago.

But things which are meant to last are often beautiful as well, and those honest red-faced laborers who worked for the glory of the Eternal God intended their work to bear witness to their piety till Judgment Day itself. Each gave his best to God: the stone-carver who could copy the toothless hollow-cheeked faces of the village grandfathers carved them for the tops of the church pillars; the woodworker carved a leaf-and-vine design into the backs of the choir stalls; the local artist painted on the back wall of the church a bright red picture of Hell, with grinning demons pitchforking sinners down into the sea of flame.

What sort of people were they who built and carved these lovely old churches? Most of them could not read or write, and there are therefore no letters or documents written by common people. One clue to the spirit of the time, however, lies in the story of Magna Carta. Magna Carta, or the Great Charter, may be called the great-great-grandfather of our American Declaration of Independence. King John, the sixth king after the Norman Conquest, went a little too far in suppressing the rights of the great lords over whom he ruled. They suddenly raised objections and before he knew exactly what was happening, they frightened him into signing a charter promising that he would not levy most kinds of taxes without their consent and also that he could not imprison or punish anyone without showing fair reasons. The grass still grows in the riverside field called Runnymede near London (*mede* for meadow; perhaps *runny* referred to floods from the Thames) where the Great Charter was signed on June 15th, 1215; and the world has yet to see the freedom which John thus gave his barons given to all men everywhere. It was some time before the common people of England won the same rights, but they took an important step in that direction just fifty years later when a man called Simon de Montfort led the people in a demand for a "parliament" or assembly in which they could express their ideas to the king. King Henry III did not like the idea and Simon was soon killed, but the next king,

Edward I, began to call representatives of the people together for frequent parliaments. Many of the laws that were passed with their approval exist in some modernized form even today.

In those days life was very hard for poor people, and most people were very poor. Sometimes a lord allowed his serfs to pay their taxes in money instead of in "work-days" which small farmers could not afford to give away from their own land. But all the same, many serfs wanted to run away from their lord and try to earn a living somewhere else. Their chance came when England was swept by terrible epidemics. No one knows exactly how many people died of the plague; historians think it may have been as many as half the people in the country. Whole families were wiped out. It was impossible to give the bodies private burial and they were simply dumped into "plague pits." From the thirteenth to the sixteenth century, these epidemics occurred every now and then, with the same dreadful conditions repeated each time. It is said that one reason why the boys at a famous London school have a large cricket field in the middle of the city is that victims of the plague were buried there and no one wished to build houses on or near the unhappy spot. Be that as it may, the open space proved very useful during World War II when it made an excellent site for trench shelters, anti-aircraft guns and barrage balloons.

Though many died of the plague, it brought good fortune to those who were lucky enough to survive it. There was soon such a shortage of men on the land that if a serf ran away from his lord and pretended to be a freeman somewhere else, no one asked too many questions about his past. Wages rose, and for some time men did not feel the loss of their own little strips of land. When wages fell, later on, the people, who had begun to realize that they had a certain amount of power, marched angrily to London and captured the whole city, fortress Tower, high walls and all. Naturally the lords and ladies, clergy and learned men feared that the peasants would murder them and loot the city. The fourteen-year-old king, Richard II, bravely went out to meet the peasants alone and broke the rebellion by promising them many of the things they asked for—a set rent to take the place of workdays, liberation acts to set serfs free, pardons for the rebels. Richard really wanted to be a democratic king, leader of the common people rather than of the aristocrats. Unfortunately he was unable to keep his promises, for the barons had no intention of forgiving the peasants who had frightened them so badly, and instead of being pardoned, Wat Tyler and the other peasant leaders were killed, and the liberation acts were torn up. King Richard himself was soon murdered. With his death the people of England lost their last chance for hundreds of years of ruling the country through their king.

Meanwhile, England was really ruled by a fairly small wealthy and aristocratic governing class, and though it was always possible for a poor man to work his way up into that class if he were lucky enough, very few actually succeeded in doing so. Sometimes the people wanted to change the system. At other periods they were content with things as they were. So little was Shakespeare interested in democracy, for instance, that when he wrote a play about King John he made no reference to Magna Carta, and when he wrote about Richard II he did not mention the Peasants' Uprising and Richard's attempt to become the peasants' leader.

But two hundred years were yet to pass before Shakespeare was to write what many people consider the greatest poetry in the world. Meanwhile, the first great English poet had been born in London, in 1340 or '41. Geoffrey Chaucer receives less honor in our day than is his due only because the English language has changed so much in the six hundred years since he made it a literary tongue. The modern reader is more likely to notice Chaucer's strange spellings and unfamiliar words than the depth of his wisdom or the subtlety of his humor. Much of his poetry is as difficult to read as if it were written in a foreign language:

"I herde a swogh that gan aboute renne;"

On the other hand, passages frequently come down to us with their original vigor undiminished by time or change; for example, Chaucer's alphabetic prayer to the Holy Virgin:

> "Glorious mayde and moder, which that never
> Were bitter, neither in erthe nor in see,
> But ful of swetnesse and of mercy ever
> Help that my fader be not wroth with me!"

Sometimes Chaucer is hard to understand because he belonged, after all, to the Middle Ages, and we cannot put ourselves back into the world which he knew. On the other hand, because he was very well educated, much traveled, a very shrewd judge of people and a lover of humanity in all ranks, there are times when he seems closer to us in feeling than many men of later ages.

Chaucer died in 1400. During the following century, there was a long civil war called the Wars of the Roses, between the supporters of rival claimants to the throne. The common people paid little attention to the struggle, but the barons bled themselves white, and as a result the feudal system passed away. By the time King Henry VII came to the throne in 1485 English farmers and craftsmen had learned how to produce more food and clothing, the population had begun to increase rapidly as a result, and England was ready for the great event that was eventually to transform her into a modern democracy.

CHAPTER TEN

Tudor and Stuart England
1485—1640

THE discovery of America is the great landmark that divides modern times from the Middle Ages. Hundreds of thousands of Americans, from Pocahontas and Ben Franklin to the "G.I. Joes" of World War II, have tiptoed around the lovely tomb of Henry VII and his wife, Elizabeth of York, in the center of Henry's jewel-like chapel in Westminster Abbey. But few among them remembered Henry's eager interest in the land from which they had come. Even before Columbus reached the West Indies in 1492 ships had sailed westward from Bristol in search of lands the sailors had heard about when they visited Iceland, where Leif Erikson's voyages were still remembered. It was Henry VII himself who encouraged John Cabot to make his first voyage from England to Nova Scotia and Newfoundland in 1497, and to attempt a second. This time John Cabot and his sailors disappeared, and Spain and Portugal took the lead in the international race for new wealth and power. Nevertheless, as the sixteenth century went on, not only did England acquire experience in trans-Atlantic navigation and knowledge of the New World, but her commercial development at home was greater than that of France or Holland. This gave her an advantage in the contest later on.

It was exciting to live in England in the sixteenth and seventeenth centuries. New ideas were in the air. Not only was the world larger than people had imagined; England itself was changing. There were new developments in politics, in culture, in religion. Because Henry VII did not want the old nobility to regain the strength it had lost during the Wars of the Roses, he was letting political power fall into the hands of new men of the middle classes. He chose them well, for although there was no standing army and no police system, the country was for the most part peaceful and well-behaved. This too was an age of scientific experimentation which led to the important discoveries of later centuries—Newton's law of gravitation and the invention of microscopes and telescopes, for instance.

But the change which loomed largest in the minds of many of the people at the time was the change in England's state religion. Hitherto, England had been a Roman Catholic country and both rulers and people had remained firm in their loyalty to the Church. Both King Henry VII and King Henry VIII ordered unbelievers to be burned at the stake, for in those days "freedom of religion" would have been regarded by most people as an invention of the devil himself to tempt weaklings away from the True Faith. Henry VIII was awarded the title, "Defender of the Faith," by the Pope; in view of what happened later it is odd that these words are still stamped on British coins.

For it was Henry VIII who led England away from the Pope. Not that he objected to the Catholic creed; on the contrary, he retained it unchanged when he established his own church in England. But Henry wanted a son to inherit the throne, and his wife had borne him only a daughter. At that time no woman had ever ruled and Henry was not sure that his daughter would be accepted as queen. So he decided that he must have a new wife, and he appealed to the Pope to dissolve his marriage on the ground that a marriage between his brother's widow and himself was not valid. The Pope refused, and Henry in anger and stubborn determination to have his way decided that henceforth the Pope would have no power in England and the head of the English Church would be the king. Fate played a joke on him after all this, for although in the end he married six times, his only son died young after a brief reign, and not only were his two daughters accepted as queens, but one of them, Elizabeth, became one of the greatest of England's monarchs.

Of course Henry could not have won the approval of Parliament to his action, as he had to do, if it had not been true that many people in England resented the strength of the Pope and the ever-increasing wealth of the Roman Church. It was because the king received the strong support of the majority of the people that this great movement of the Reformation took place without much bloodshed and bitter strife. Parliament remained in session for six years, passing the laws necessary for the establishment of the national church and for the disposal of the enormous wealth and vast estates that had belonged to the Roman Catholic Church and that were now seized by the State. One-fifth of all the land in England had belonged to the Church, much of it being the property of the great monasteries. These were broken up and the monks and priests scattered. Some went over to the English Church; some spent the rest of their lives in hiding. Much of the church land was sold to farmers who were more interested in its productivity than the monks had been. In growing more food and wool they increased their own wealth and added to the resources of the country. Meanwhile, with the money derived from the sale of the land Henry built a great navy and paid for one of the many wars with France.

Not that there was no opposition at all to the King's action. In the North of England there was an uprising in 1536, and for years to come rebellious sons of loyal Catholic families were imprisoned in the Tower or had their heads cut off for "treasonable" activity against the king. Among them was Sir Thomas More, who was one of the greatest of all Englishmen.

But there were other important results from the reign of Henry VIII. It was at this time that Wales became politically a part of England. For centuries there had been intermittent fighting between the Welsh and the "Marcher Lords," English nobles whose estates lay along the border of Wales. The Marcher Lords gradually conquered most of Wales and reigned there as independent chieftains. During the Wars of the Roses, however, they went off to fight in England itself, and most of them were killed in the battles for the throne. As a result, their castles and estates were inherited by the State, and Henry, who was, as it happened, a Welshman himself, decided that the time had come when Wales could be united with England. Since the Welsh were very proud of having one of their own people on the throne of England he was able to count on their loyal support. Wales quickly settled down under English law and justice, though she keeps her own language, customs and culture.

Henry VIII died in 1547 and was followed by his young son, Edward VI. Edward soon died and was succeeded by Henry's daughter Mary, who had remained Catholic and who now beheaded Protestants for a change. Meanwhile, ordinary people were more interested in the houses they lived in, the food they ate and the clothes they wore than in these political changes, however startling they seem to us.

Many farmers today live in houses that were built when Henry VIII was king, though the number of people living in the house may have changed greatly. The solid brick or stone "cottages," with their tiny windows and their walls three feet thick, sometimes housed three large families back in the sixteenth century. Each family had a single moderately large kitchen-dining-living-room and a single bedroom of the same size just above it. Water was carried from the village well; often there were no sanitary arrangements at all. Later on, the number of families was sometimes reduced to two, so that each had an extra room. And in the twentieth century, many an ancient cottage has come into the hands of a single small family which, at considerable expense, has added modern plumbing and electricity, enlarged the windows, turned one of the old kitchens with its enormous fireplace into a modern living-room, and thus managed to keep some of the charm of old things while adding modern comfort.

But not all sixteenth-century houses were four- or six-room cottages. Shortly before the king ordered the monasteries to be broken up there had been a fashion for fine building and for fine decoration in churches, monks' dining-halls and the private lodgings of the abbots or priors who were in charge of the monasteries. When the church property was sold by the king, the gentleman farmers who bought the lands and buildings usually kept the abbot's lodging as part of the house which they built for themselves on the site. So the houses in which wealthy people lived gradually changed from bare fortified castles with straw on the cold stone floors, only a large draughty two-storied hall in which to eat and sleep, and little in the way of ornament. There was no longer a need for fortress homes, so the gentry and the nobility imitated the monks and had large bay windows in their new houses. Bedrooms and parlors were built, as well as the hall. There were skilfully wrought balustrades for their stairs and quaintly designed firebacks of Sussex iron for their fireplaces. Fine hand-carved oak paneling or tapestries covered the walls. Except in kitchens and sculleries, the floors were of beautifully laid oak. In the largest houses a minstrel gallery was built at one end of the dining-hall, so that my lord might enjoy music at his meals; from the floor to the gallery there was a wooden screen carved by local craftsmen or by imported Italian artists, as the state of the master's purse might decree. But the time was passing when craftsmen co-operated so closely in designing a house and in building it that no single man could claim the honor of conceiving the plan for the finished work. The craftsmen's guilds of the Middle Ages were losing their strength and unity, and the architect who now began to plan buildings and their decoration was not one of the gang of workers on the job as the master builders had been before him.

Even finer than the hundreds of Tudor mansions still in use in England are the public buildings of the period: the churches that were built or enlarged just before the Reformation, the college buildings at the universities of Oxford and Cambridge, the market halls, the royal palaces in whose great mirrored galleries ordinary citizens now loiter, admiring the views of formal gardens once reserved for the pleasure of kings.

With such examples of fine architecture and furnishings before them—houses with well-proportioned rooms, walls and floors so thick as to be nearly soundproof, cupboards large enough to contain the annual produce of the locality when it was stored away in the autumn, fittings of hand-turned brass that might well be displayed in museums as works of art—it is not surprising that the British at first looked with grave doubts upon the pre-fabricated and temporary houses constructed during the acute housing shortage resulting from the Second World War. No amount of cheap building (and there has been a great deal of it in recent times) had obscured their ideal, and their ideal in housing was a high one. They wanted the conveniences of a modern kitchen, but they also wanted the fine proportions, the sound construction, the spaciousness and the sense of permanence that characterized their traditional building.

The sixteenth and seventeenth centuries, like our own, were a period when good and evil were very closely intermingled. When farmers obtained permission to put fences around pieces of "common land" on which the villagers had pastured their livestock for centuries, the immediate result was a good one, for cultivating the well-fertilized common pastures increased the amount of food in the country. On the other hand, thousands of small farmers soon spent the money they received for their grazing rights, and having become landless laborers, soon found themselves in city slums. As the population of England increased, more and more food was demanded. Prices rose, and more of the common land was fenced off, legally or otherwise, for the growing of wheat. While successful large-scale farmers became richer and richer, more and more villagers went out on the roads. No wonder 7200 thieves were hanged during the thirty-eight-year reign of Henry VIII. Probably many of them were parents caught stealing bread for their children. Nor is it surprising to find that already in 1572 England had to raise money by taxation for the support of the poor; a very famous Poor Law was passed in Queen Elizabeth's reign, setting up "Work

Houses" in which people who could not support themselves lived and worked under parish supervision.

There were other evils that came out of this period. Queen Elizabeth, like other rulers of England, treated conquered Ireland in much the same way as white settlers treated the Indians in North America. Ireland had been conquered long ago but the Irish had not settled down easily to being ruled by foreigners. So Scottish and English Protestant "colonists" were given lands in Ireland and Ireland's trade was controlled to please England. The result was that the Irish, who had been prosperous before, became a very poor people. Naturally they learned to hate the English with a hatred that is only now dying away.

Nowadays the Scottish and the English realize that their ancestors behaved very cruelly in the sixteenth and seventeenth centuries and at the worst of the rebellious periods since, and are sorry about it. On the other hand, they do not know how to make amends without doing injury to innocent people, any more than Americans could make amends to the Indians by giving their land back or to the Negroes who suffered in slave ships by shipping them back to Africa. The Protestants in Ireland have been there for three hundred years; they could not be moved out without much injustice or without disrupting the entire life of the country. Most of them live in Northern Ireland and are content that Northern Ireland be governed as a part of the United Kingdom, for they cling to their ties with England and Scotland. The majority of the people in Southern Ireland (Eire) are of Catholic Irish stock; not only is their country independent but they would like to have Northern Ireland united with them and independent as well. Eire remained neutral rather than help Britain during the war. However, tens of thousands of Irish citizens, some of whom approved the stand their government had taken officially, nevertheless crossed the Irish Sea as individuals and joined the British forces.

There are many people who feel that if any nation ever had a "Golden Age," England's came while Queen Elizabeth was on the throne. Elizabeth ruled from 1558 to 1603, and though there was poverty among sections of her people, her reign saw a tremendous increase in the country's wealth, knowledge and power.

Not that Elizabeth had an easy time being queen. England was weak compared with Spain. England was officially Protestant again but there were many Catholics who wished to see a Catholic monarch on the throne in order that the kingdom might be brought back to the Catholic Church. Elizabeth's cousin, Mary Stuart, Queen of Scots, was a Catholic and had some claim to the throne; both the English Catholics and Spain hoped to see Elizabeth out of the way and Mary Stuart as queen. It was not yet too late to recover for the Church the property confiscated by Elizabeth's father.

Elizabeth knew her own position was dangerous but for a long time she did little about it. Mary Stuart was driven off the throne of Scotland; she fled to England, where her presence alone was a threat to Elizabeth's power. Elizabeth therefore ordered her imprisonment, though the conditions of her detention were easy and Mary had her own servants and all the comforts befitting a queen. As long as she was alive, however, there were plots to kill Elizabeth and make Mary Queen of England. At last, in 1587, one more plot was discovered, with Mary very much involved, and Elizabeth sentenced her to death. Mary, forty-five years old and no longer lovely as she had been in her romantic youth, died as bravely as anyone in history. On the day before she went to the scaffold she wrote a letter to her brother-in-law, the King of France; her handwriting, fine and pointed and very easy to read, betrays no failing of the spirit that had sustained her through seventeen years of imprisonment.

But Elizabeth's troubles had not ended. Until now King Philip of Spain had not declared war on England despite religious differences and constant raiding and rivalry at sea, because hitherto he had hoped that someone would murder Elizabeth, Mary would become queen, and England would become a Catholic ally without his having to do anything. Now Mary was gone and Philip dec he could no longer waste any time. So he ordered a great fleet of wooden ships to be fitted out and within a year the Spanish Armada sailed northward for the conquest of England. It was July 1588 before it got there, and then the battle began.

Unfortunately for the Spanish, the admirals who planned their invasion had not kept up-to-date in their ideas of naval warfare. They expected to fight a war at sea exactly like a war on land, with soldiers boarding each other's craft and fighting in single combat until one side or the other had captured most of the ships. That was the way in which wars had always been fought at sea.

But in the sixteenth century, the English and the Dutch had learned a new kind of sea warfare. They had built small fast ships, mounted guns below deck as well as on top, cut down the number of fighting men they carried, and developed the art of swinging their ships around very rapidly, whatever the direction of the wind. The Spanish had no chance to grapple and board these darting enemy vessels. The English bombarded the lumbering Spanish galleons from a distance until their ammunition ran short; then they rushed in to set them on fire, withdrawing before the soldiers jammed together on the Spanish decks could begin to fight. The rest of the Armada was driven up the Channel, scattered by gales and wrecked on the west coasts of Scotland and Ireland as the survivors tried to make their way southward again. England had lost less than one hundred men.

The defeat of the Armada was a turning point in English history. The battle had been won for the Queen, but not by her; it was the merchant marine, not the small Royal Navy, which defeated Spain. The ordinary middle-class traders who shipped their wool abroad and imported tobacco and sugar and silk looked at themselves with new respect. And when the next two kings, James I and Charles I, claimed that they ruled by divine right and tried to reduce the power of Parliament, the folk who had known how to handle the Armada decided they knew how to handle a tyrant as well.

But it was not the defeat of the Armada which was the greatest glory of the Elizabethan Age. Nor was it the great Queen herself. Elizabeth Tudor's political sense was far overshadowed by the genius of her subject, William Shakespeare. Shakespeare's understanding of the range of human feeling appears more miraculous as the centuries go by, and in comment appropriate to any current crisis he continues to surpass in human understanding the writers actually on the scene. English schoolchildren who traditionally present Shakespeare as their annual school play have to work very much harder on their production than American youngsters doing a modern farce. But they carry away in their memory speeches whose meaning deepens with the passage of time and the growth of experience.

CHAPTER ELEVEN

The British and the American Revolutions
1640—1815

MOST great countries have had a revolution. It seems to be one of the steps the common people have had to take in order to share in the good things of life. France and the United States had theirs a long time ago, in 1789 and 1776. For some reason, the term "British Revolution" is not used ordinarily, but the British had a revolution all the same, and theirs was the earliest of all. It started in 1640.

In the British Revolution, there was, of course, no question of winning national independence. Otherwise, the similarity between the British and the American revolutions is very close. The American slogan was "No taxation without representation" because the colonists realized that whoever taxed them really ruled the land; they intended to keep that power in their own hands rather than let it cross the sea to Parliament in England. In 1640 the King thought he ought to have the right to levy taxes; Parliament said No, realizing, as the Americans did later, that if Parliament could hold the purse strings Parliament would hold the power. Whereas the wise Queen Elizabeth had preserved her popularity with Parliament by keeping her expenses as small as possible, Charles I believed that he ruled by divine right and could therefore call for as much money as he liked.

Long before the war actually broke out, he began to meet with difficulties. In 1628 he asked Parliament for funds; in return for the money he received he signed a document called "The Petition of Right," promising not to imprison people unless they were charged with breaking a law and not to compel anyone to make any gifts or loans or to pay taxes to the King without the consent of Parliament. Parliament at once decided to vote taxes for his expenses a year at a time instead of for life, as had been done before. Charles became very angry. The men in Parliament found themselves in a very difficult position: if they disobeyed the King they were traitors and could be hanged; if they obeyed him they were accepting what they called tyranny and we call a dictatorship. Parliament met in a final stormy session. The Speaker tried to leave his chair so that he would not have to preside over so rebellious a meeting. His companions held him down until they had passed three resolutions against the King's party. Then Parliament dissolved. Charles swore that he could get along without Parliament or its taxes. Eleven years went by before he found it necessary to call Parliament together again.

When the new Parliament met in 1640, the times were ripe for trouble. A rebellion had broken out in Scotland, which had been united with England when the Scottish King James VI became James I of England after Elizabeth's death. Now a Scottish army had invaded England from the North, and Charles had to raise some money to pay his army to go and put down the rebels. He was ready to insist on what he considered to be his rights. But the members of Parliament were in no mood to take orders from the King. In less than two years there was civil war.

At the beginning of this war, Parliament had a great deal of money but no army; the King had a large and well-trained army under leaders who were loyal to him, but he could not pay them. As a result, Parliament lost several battles and appeared to be losing the war at first, but little by little her army learned from experience, and finally produced a great leader and general called Oliver Cromwell. Meanwhile, the King found it more and more difficult to raise funds for supplies even though his friends sold their family heirlooms to provide him with the means to continue fighting. There were good men on both sides, and men with differing views, for when war actually started some of the Parliamentary leaders switched over to the King's side because they felt they could not break their oath of allegiance to him even when they thought he was wrong.

From 1642 to 1646 the war continued. Finally, in May, 1646, the King fled to Scotland and surrendered to the Scots. Oliver Cromwell was left in a key position as the head of the army, which was chiefly composed of Puritans, and as a very important member of Parliament, which was made up mainly of Presbyterians. Because of these religious and political differences, the fate of the defeated King was uncertain for three years. Then the Presbyterians, who were more friendly to the King, were driven out of Parliament and he was brought to trial by the Puritans who were left. Convicted of treason to the State (a king could hardly be guilty of treason to himself), Charles was beheaded. The Puritans then abolished the hereditary House of Lords, leaving only the House of Commons in Parliament. England ceased to be a monarchy and became a republic known as the "Commonwealth."

Hitherto, Oliver Cromwell had been an earlier George Washington. Like Washington, he was a great land-owner. Like Washington, he first became a recognized leader among the farmers and then in political circles. Like Washington, he was a remarkable general. He fought for the same cause as Washington—government by the people's representatives rather than by an absolute monarch. But from 1649 on, his career took a very different course.

In 1649 Ireland joined in the Civil War, taking the side of the King. Cromwell and his army therefore crossed the Irish Sea to reconquer the Irish. Though they believed in the rights of the people at home they do not seem to have realized that the Irish had rights too, and treated them as harshly as any feudal lord. When the Irish war was finished, Cromwell moved north to Scotland to fight an army raised by Charles II, who had been crowned king in Edinburgh after his father's execution in London. Then Parliament declared war on Holland over trade difficulties, and when that was finished there was a war with Spain.

It would have been better for the new republic if Cromwell had been able to keep out of war, like Washington in the new American republic a hundred and thirty years later. The wars were expensive and only added to the quarrels taking place in England. One Parliament followed another. Cromwell was given the title of "Lord Protector" and ruled with the support of the army. A new Parliament came to power and set up the House of Lords once again. Finally Cromwell died in 1658 and his son, who was nicknamed "Tumbledown Dick" was named Lord Protector. The harvests were bad, as they had been at the beginning of the Revolution, and people were poor and miserable. It was not surprising that in the general disorder Charles II was invited to come back and England once more had a king on the throne.

But he was not the same sort of king as Charles I. Many people had suffered during the revolution, but it had not been fought in vain. Charles II knew that he was king of England only so long as he let Parliament have its own way. He was no king "by divine right" but only by consent of the lawyers and merchants and farmers and God-fearing businessmen who really ruled the land. Henceforth the King of England was to be a symbol, as the American flag is a symbol, of the nation, and when, in years to come, the British said "God save the King" they were to mean precisely what Americans mean when we say of the flag, "Long may it wave."

There was one more upheaval to come to England in the seventeenth century. The Catholic James II, brother of the second Charles, became king when Charles died. Religious difficulties again became important, not only because people sincerely believed that they should use every means, including force, to convert non-believers to their own true faith, but also because religious differences reflected social differences. The London working people, for instance, were Puritans while the North of England farmers were Catholics and there were many things they did not agree about besides religion. James went too far and too fast in trying to make the country Catholic again. In a very short time he was driven into exile and King William and Queen Mary came to the throne. So this so-called "Glorious Revolution" of 1688 repeated one of the lessons of the revolution in 1640: the power that had once belonged to the king was now firmly in the hands of the people, and they would have little patience with a king who would not behave as they thought he should.

But while king and Parliament quarreled bitterly and wars were fought both at home and abroad, most people went on living their ordinary lives, just as millions of people lived their ordinary lives during the greater wars of the twentieth century. What those lives were like is shown in the letters written to her fiancé by a girl called Dorothy Osborne in the 1650's, and by the diary kept by Samuel Pepys during the years 1659 to 1669. Everyone who reads Dorothy Osborne's letters falls in love with her. Dorothy and her brother were traveling on the Isle of Wight when they met a charming young man called Sir William Temple, who promptly got himself into trouble by scratching, as a joke, a political slogan on the glass of the window at the inn where they were staying. Since politics were not a subject to make jokes about in those days, young Sir William might have paid dearly for his fun. Dorothy saved him, however, by going before the local judge and taking the blame. The judge was a gallant gentleman and could not punish a lady— and such a pretty one at that. So the three young people went on very happily, William and Dorothy falling deeply in love. But it was some time before they could get married, and in the meantime, Dorothy wrote a series of letters that might still serve as models to parted lovers: "Last night I was in the garden till 11 o'clock. It was the sweetest night that e'er I saw. The garden looked so well and the jasmine smelt beyond all perfume. And yet I was not pleased. The place had all the charms it used to have when I was most satisfied with it, and had you been there I should have liked it much more than ever I did; but that not being, it was no more to me than the next field, and only served me for a place to roam in without disturbance."

Samuel Pepys is not the only great diarist of his time but he is the most revealing, both of his own character and that of his age: "SEPTEMBER 8TH, 1662: Dined at home with my wife. It being washing-day, we had a good pie baked of a leg of mutton. . . . JANUARY 6TH, 1663: This morning I began a practice, which I find, by the ease I do it with, that I shall continue, it saving money and time; that is, to trimme myself with a razer: which pleases me mightily. . . . SEPTEMBER 4TH, 1665: Walked home, my Lord Brouncker giving me a very neat cane to walk with; but it troubled me to pass by Coome farme, where about twenty-one people have died of the plague. . . . OCTOBER 26, 1665: Sir Christopher Mings and I together by water to the Tower; and I find him a very witty, well-spoken fellow, and mighty free to tell his parentage, being a shoemaker's son. . . . DECEMBER 1ST, 1665: All the day long shut up in my little closet at my office. Then home by promise to my wife, to have mirth there. So we had our neighbours, little Miss Tooker and Mrs. Daniels, to dance, and after supper, I to bed and left them merry below, which they did not part from till two or three in the morning."

Meanwhile, all through this century, important events were taking place on the Atlantic seaboard of North America. In 1608 the colony at Jamestown, Virginia, was started; in 1620, the Pilgrims landed at Plymouth Rock after having drawn up, on shipboard, the document called the "Mayflower Compact," in which they agreed to govern themselves by democratic methods. The Pilgrims, in common with other sects, had suffered for their religion in England, and they left the mother country before Cromwell's Puritans ruled the land. But they brought with them to America something which, out of all the civilized nations in the world, only one country could give them, and that was their understanding of the principles of self-government. In 1620 England still had a long way to go before she could call herself a democracy, but she had been moving step by step in that direction ever since

King John signed Magna Carta in 1215, and the Pilgrims had the benefit of that three hundred and fifty years of experience.

But if it is possible to explain to some extent the political wisdom of the American colonists, there is no explanation except that of magnificent courage to tell how they endured the change from the reasonable physical comfort which even poor people had in England to the bitter hardships of life in the first colonies. England's climate is gentle and kind, people's houses were solidly built of brick or stone and were furnished with good oak furniture handed down from generation to generation. The shops around the village green were well stocked; the local craftsmen were skilful workers and good neighbors. There was no necessity in England for a man to be a Jack-of-all-trades. The first English colonists did not even know how to build log cabins for they had never seen cabins in England. Fortunately they were willing to learn from the Swedes who soon arrived in Delaware.

For the next hundred and fifty years, while the colonists grew in numbers, worked hard and prospered despite their difficulties, people in England persisted in regarding the colonies merely as a source of benefit to the mother country. However, for a long time the colonists managed to do pretty much what they liked and trouble really started only when Britain decided to enforce some of the laws which had long been on the books but which no one had obeyed. At that moment the question of who controlled the purse—and therefore governed the land—became of vital importance, just as it had in the earlier British revolution. Both sides realized the importance of the question and there were not many voices raised even among the radicals in Britain in favor of the colonial point of view. A few spoke up, both in Parliament and outside, but most members of Parliament regarded it as a law of nature that colonies should pay taxes levied by the motherland. It was shocking to discover that the colonists in America believed in another "law of nature" which was self-government even for colonists. American history books used to call King George III a

Canterbury Cathedral from the old city gate

The men folks meet for a pint and a good argument in the old village pu

Modern county council houses for low-income families

Three generations of a typical English family have tea together on Sunday

An example of modern school architecture in Kent

Modern boys in an ancient public school, Christ Hospital, London

The farmyard gate on a typical English farm

On market days sheep have the right of way in the High Street

British schoolboys playing cricket

Bodiam Castle with moat and drawbridge near Hastings in Sussex

A new motor highway with cycle path in southern England

The Tower of London and Tower Bridge

The Nelson monument in Trafalgar Square at Whitehall, the heart of the British Empire

Salisbury Cathedral, the tallest spire in England, from the River Avon

Lands End, Cornwall

Many buildings in the shadow of St. Paul's Cathedral were destroyed
by Nazi fire bombs in 1940

London sees some ancient pageantry when the Queen drives in the Golden State Coach
to open Parliament

The half-timbered village of Woebley in Herefordshire

The great Roman Wall near Housesteads, Northumberland

The ancient town of Ludlow in Shropshire

Queen Elizabeth II and the Duke of Edinburgh

tyrant—as of course he was called in the propaganda of the time—but the King of England no longer had power, as such, and George III acquired his influence only by becoming a very shrewd politician. It was Parliament, not the King, who made the vital decisions concerning the colonies.

Just as there had been many in the Civil War of 1640 who opposed the King's ideas but could not bring themselves to commit treason by fighting against him, so there were many in the American colonies who tried very hard to find a way of avoiding actual war against the Crown. Benjamin Franklin talked to everyone he met in London, explaining the colonial point of view, and then came back and for a while tried to explain the London point of view to the colonists. At one time, Alexander Hamilton, who later became the first American Secretary of the Treasury, suggested a scheme which would have made the colonies legally independent but attached to the Crown just as a dozen countries, including Canada, Australia, New Zealand and South Africa are independent but a part of the British Commonwealth today. And when war finally broke out, thousands of hard-working, honest and prosperous Americans who felt that they could not rebel against their king, fled to Canada, leaving their homes and property eventually to be confiscated.

The story of the Revolutionary War and of the magnificent solution which the colonists found to the problems of the peace that followed needs no retelling. Before the struggle had ended, Britain was at war with Spain, France and Holland as well as her rebellious colonies, for this was a trade war as well as a war for political ideals.

Having lost the war, she took the lesson it taught to heart. Very reluctantly at first but with a growing sense of obligation, Britain granted independence to her Dominions and began to plan for increasing self-government and final independence for the colonies as well. Unlike tyranny, which can only become more tyrannical, British policy, based deep down on democratic ideals, steadily became more democratic.

Every British school child is taught to admire and respect George Washington as one of the great men of world history. Washington's statue stands in Trafalgar Square, one of the main centers of London life. (A statue of a later American hero, Abraham Lincoln, stands near the Houses of Parliament.) But though most Americans are gratified to find that the British are very fair in their treatment of the American Revolution, they are often shocked to discover that their friends in England do not even know that there was a War of 1812 between the United States and Britain. What to the Americans was "The War of 1812" was to the British only a minor campaign in the long-continued war against Napoleon, and the British were far more interested in Napoleon's final battles and defeat on the Continent than they were in a quarrel about the Canadian-U. S. boundary, the methods they had used in enforcing a blockade of Europe and the impressment of seamen.

The American Revolution had been followed by the French Revolution in 1789. In France, England and the other countries of Europe had seen with fear and horror, all the violence of mob rule. The common people of France, however, hoped to see risings of the people in other countries too, and their army went forth to fight those whom they regarded not only as their own enemies but the enemies of common people everywhere. However, before the wars were over, Napoleon had risen from the ranks and had become not only the commander-in-chief of the French army but the dictator of France. In 1805 the British fully expected him to invade Britain. Coastal defenses were built and home guards called out. But the invasion did not take place. Instead the one-armed sea-captain, Horatio Nelson, defeated the French Navy in the battle of Trafalgar; and Napoleon's land strategy led to the disastrous Russian campaign which cost him an army. Finally defeated at Waterloo in 1815, Napoleon was sentenced by the British to captivity on the island of St. Helena in the South Atlantic, and died there in 1821, six years after his defeat.

CHAPTER TWELVE

The Nineteenth and Twentieth Centuries

HAVE you ever wondered why it was that for thousands of years the ways in which human beings obtained their food, provided their clothing and built their homes did not change very much, and then in less than a century the whole pattern was changed and the age of inventions was upon us? Why was it that men who were capable of reaching the highest levels of artistic and intellectual development continued to produce by hand their clothes, their household equipment, the goods they sold abroad? Why was the modern factory not invented by the ancient Greeks or the Romans? Why was there such a long gap between the invention of agriculture, which changed men from wandering hunters to citizens of a settled community, and the invention of modern machinery which resulted in the "Industrial Revolution"?

The answer to those questions can be given very briefly. Until recent times there was no demand for mass production. Furthermore, until recent times there was not enough wealth available to create a system of mass production even if the demand for it had arisen. If you want to start a factory you have to have money; obviously it took a great deal of money to change England from a farming country into a manufacturing one. The Industrial Revolution started in England, and England invented the modern industrial system because it happened that in the eighteenth and early nineteenth centuries England needed mass production and had sufficient wealth ready for use to pay for the development of the new system.

What the Industrial Revolution meant was that for the first time in history a community did not have to be self-supporting. Except for a few luxuries like spices and silk, people had hitherto produced everything they needed in their own district. A village or a country town had contained craftsmen of all sorts—bakers who made bread from local grain ground by their friend, the miller, shoemakers and saddlers who used local leather, spinsters who spun and websters who wove the wool from their neighbor's herds of sheep, wheelwrights and cartwrights who made wooden wheels and carts. All of these people had worked in their own homes or shops, keeping a pig or a cow and raising a few vegetables in their gardens. Now people stopped working at home, the variety of crafts disappeared, and crowded factory towns grew up, with their thousands of men, women and children chiefly occupied in producing only one type of thing. Before, each man had been his own "boss." Now thousands worked for a man they might never see.

Strangely enough, the change really started with the farmers. During most of the history of the human race most people in the world had not had enough to eat, and as a result, many babies died in infancy and comparatively few people survived to old age. But when the English farmers began to experiment with crop rotation and other new methods of raising food, the people in Britain began to get enough food, fewer babies died, disease became less prevalent and the population increased very rapidly. So there was a sudden need for more clothes than could easily be woven by hand. At the same time British ships were sailing across the ocean carrying goods produced in Britain and coming back eager for more. Merchants were becoming very rich through their overseas trade. Many of them bought land and built themselves fine country homes but when they had bought all the land they wanted and built their houses, they still had money left over. It was hard to know what to do with it. Savings banks had not been invented; other means of investment were limited by the lack of things to buy or sell. Furthermore, in addition to all these factors which were bound to have their effect on social progress, there were constant wars which created a demand for large supplies of equipment. Armies began to wear special uniforms, to carry standardized weapons. What was badly needed was some way of making things very much more quickly, to satisfy all the needs both of people in England and of people outside. At the same time it was clearly desirable that people who had money should have a chance to put it to use.

Many people in Britain realized all this and set to work to try to invent the new machines that were needed. That is why so many of the basic machines of the modern age were invented in England: the steam engine by James Watt, the steam locomotive by Trevithick, the steam turbine by Sir Charles Parsons, the flying shuttle by Kay, the spinning jenny by Hargreaves, the power loom by Cartwright. Methods of smelting iron by using coal were perfected in England; and since greater production of goods meant that there was need for better means of transport, engineers soon invented new methods of digging canals, laying roads, building bridges and railroads. It is not strange that Charles Dickens and other English visitors to the United States complained bitterly of American "corduroys"; they were used to the macadam highways of England. When the steamship was invented by the American, Robert Fulton, British seamen recognized its importance, and before long not only were three-fourths of the ships that sailed the seas British ships, but nine-tenths of those driven by steam were British. Almost overnight England had developed a talent for mechanics which turned every new idea to good account.

Factories sprang up by the hundreds and thousands, in the north as well as in the south of England. New cities came into existence. Ships went out to the far corners of the earth carrying products labeled "British Made" and came back loaded with food which was no longer being produced in sufficient quantity on England's own fertile fields. The little island of Britain became the greatest industrial center in the world, and because it was the first in the field, it became the wealthiest. But Britain did not acquire her wealth or her prestige as a nation for nothing. The people who went to work in the new factories paid very dearly for it.

Because England was the first industrial country, she made all the mistakes that people make when they start doing things a new way. Farm workers had been used to working from sunrise to sunset and longer. The first factory hands were expected to do the same because factory owners did not realize that although men can put in a long day's work, with breaks for rest, out-of-doors, they cannot do dreary factory jobs in dark stuffy sheds for sixteen hours on end. In the same way, children had always had to work, the girls helping with the family spinning, weaving, sewing or churning, while the boys were apprenticed early. Neither factory owners nor parents realized at once how great was the difference between putting a ten-year-old girl to work helping her mother with the spinning at home and having that ten-year-old shut up in a mine or a factory twelve hours a day. Thousands of children were condemned to such an existence at the beginning of the factory era; factory operators wanted them because they could be paid less than grown-ups (an evil that still exists with regard to teen-age workers in Britain), and parents put them to work because their own wages were so small that they could not afford to live without having the aid of as many children as they could raise.

As time went on, the workers formed trade unions and by going on strike again and again, forced their employers to concede shorter hours and better wages. A little more than a hundred years ago the first Factory Act was passed, forbidding women and children to work more than ten hours a day—a law which resulted in the reduction of men's hours to ten a day as well. But children and women were still allowed to work in the coal mines and little boy chimney-sweeps were employed to crawl down chimneys as late as in 1871. For a long time people who fought against such cruel social conditions were considered wicked radicals. While many great charitable organizations were founded to help the poor in England at this time, including the Salvation Army, and the Y.M.C.A. and

Y.W.C.A., most people believed that God intended each person to live his life in the position into which he had been born and that it was a defiance of His will for a miner's son, for instance, to refuse to go into the mine, however horrible conditions there might be.

But there were always many people who escaped the evils of the new factory era by leaving the country. Since Britain was an island they could not escape, like Americans a bit later, by seeking virgin territory within their own boundaries. Someone has said that Americans found their "Empire" across a river (the Mississippi) while the British had to go across the ocean. The Yankees who were dissatisfied with life at home moved westward to California; the British went to Canada, South Africa, Australia, New Zealand, and to the United States as well. The people who settled the American West included some of the finest and some of the worst characters in our history; the British Empire was built by the same kinds of people for the same mixture of reasons.

Those who could not or did not wish to leave England saw a slow but real improvement in the lives of most of the people during the nineteenth century. It is true that wheat farmers had a bad time when American grain first came on the market in large quantities and was sold more cheaply than home-grown wheat could be. Except in wartime they have feared outside competition ever since. There was another bad patch, this one affecting the cotton workers of Lancashire, during the American Civil War, when the mills had to close down because they had no cotton to spin. Eventually some cotton was produced in Egypt but many a mill family had already gone hungry. Nevertheless, in spite of local problems of this type and occasional periods of widespread unemployment, the standard of living rose all through the century.

England was divided in its opinions with regard to the American War of 1860–65. Wealthy people generally favored the South; they included the big land-owners who had close ties of friendship with the plantation owners, and the owners of the cotton mills who had close business ties with them. The common people whole-heartedly regarded the war as one for democracy and took sides with the North.

Long before the American war broke out, England had made up her mind concerning the institution of slavery. In Britain itself slavery had died out in the Norman period but there were many slaves in British territories overseas at the beginning of the nineteenth century. Largely due to the leadership of a man called William Wilberforce, all slaves in British territories were set free in 1833 and their owners were compensated in cash to the extent of £20,000,000. This was paid by the taxpayers in Britain though the slaves were held chiefly in the West Indies.

Not only were the British people interested enough in the abolition of slavery to pay for making it possible, but many were in sympathy with the South Americans then engaged in their own struggle for independence, and considerable numbers of volunteers went out to help Bolívar and San Martín in their fight against Spanish domination. Yet the British were far from having real democracy at home.

It was true that the country was governed by an elected Parliament rather than by a hereditary monarch, but very few people could vote. Women, of course, could not vote at all until 1918, and in the early 1800's male voters had to be owners of considerable property. Furthermore, Parliament was not even representative within these limits. No provision ever had been made for revising the representation in accordance with the changes in population as changes are made when our tenth-year census shows them to be necessary. Since the Industrial Revolution some formerly large towns had lost most of their population but could still send two members each to the House of Commons. Other towns had grown up in what had been sparsely inhabited farming districts and they could send no representatives at all.

This was clearly unfair and undemocratic but, as might be expected, the members who were elected by one or two farmers in the "rotten boroughs" fought any measures which would result in their losing their positions. So the effort to pass a bill to reform Parliament resulted in tremendous argument and excitement throughout the country for several years. Finally the Reform Bill was passed in 1832. The "rotten boroughs" lost their members and were merged with larger districts while new cities were given fair representation. Property qualifications were lowered so that more people could vote; later they were removed entirely. Members of Parliament were paid salaries; they had been expected to serve without pay in the past and the result had been that they were tempted to accept bribes simply to cover their living expenses.

In 1837 began the long reign of Victoria, who became Queen when she was eighteen and who lived to celebrate her Diamond Jubilee or sixtieth anniversary on the throne. A queen but not a ruler in the sense in which Elizabeth had ruled, Victoria was like her predecessor in being so typical of her own period that it is usually given her name: the Victorian Age. Symbolized by her, the British people (and to a considerable extent, the Americans as well) became more prim, serious-minded, dignified, thrifty and pious than they had ever been before. No place on earth was less merry than "Merrie England" on a Victorian Sunday.

Except in literature, Victorianism has come to denote not only primness but bad taste. You have only to look at the architecture of the period to understand why. When Victoria came to the throne, builders were still following the old rules of proportion and the houses they built were still very beautiful. Indeed, in the building of houses, the laying out of streets and the construction of the city of Bath, eighteenth-century architects had reached what many people consider the highest point in domestic architecture attained up to the present. But in the middle of Victoria's reign, builders and architects suddenly threw away all the old rules. Instead, they began to build houses in imitation of Greek temples or Chinese pagodas or even combinations of both. Like a woman wearing five pairs of beads and a dozen bracelets, a Victorian house blossomed out in Gothic towers, cupolas, fancy fretwork, colored tiles and bits of stained glass. The cheaper the house, the cheaper the ornament; no one dreamed of leaving it off altogether. Instead, because the population was still increasing very rapidly, English cities were filled with streets and streets of ugly buildings, put up as rapidly as possible. (So were many newly founded cities in America, for they came under the same influence.)

Some districts in England soon became slums. Others remained respectable though they were no less hideous. Slum-clearance schemes and new housing plans were going forward under both local and national government control when World War II interrupted them. In 1940 and '41 bombs crashed down on new-model apartment houses and on carefully designed housing estates in which low-income families could rent well-equipped, roomy, six-room apartments or houses at rents of two or three dollars a week. The set-back was disappointing, but at the same time, the bombs smashed miles of streets lined with dreary Victorian houses which ought to have been torn down years ago. For decades to come there was to be a housing shortage in England and people were going to have to make the best of overcrowded conditions and temporary makeshifts. But at least there was a greater opportunity than there had been for a hundred years to bring beauty back into England's industrial cities.

During Victoria's reign Britain fought the Crimean War (1854–56) against Russia and the Boer War (1899–1902) against the Dutch settlers in South Africa. The Crimean War would be largely forgotten today if it were not for two things: first, it was the first war in which a newspaper correspondent reported by telegraph exactly what was happening on the battlefield—and the last in which a reporter could do so without having his despatches censored; second, it was due to the unswerving persistence of Florence Nightingale that the medical services of the army that fought the Crimean War were completely reorganized and nursing became a highly skilled and respected profession for women.

The Boer War weighed heavily on the conscience of many people in Britain at the time because it was a war for more territory. Britain won, but to make up for the injustices she had committed she gave the Union of South Africa complete independence within four years after the end of hostilities. As a result of that act of justice, the leaders of the Boers, and particularly the great statesman Jan Smuts, became loyal friends of Britain and led their country both in 1914 and in 1939 to the aid of their former enemy.

Hitherto, the greatest and most costly war of all history had been the American Civil War. But when Queen Victoria died in 1901, the future was already shadowed by the possibility of war in Europe. Germany had already made one effort to obtain more power and had acquired Alsace-Lorraine. France and other countries in Europe were afraid that she would want more territory; Britain was afraid that Germany might become powerful enough at sea to threaten her own naval supremacy. The British knew only too well that their lives depended on overseas shipping, for they produced at home only a portion of the food they needed. The rest was imported from the United States, Canada, Australia, South Africa, Argentina, the West Indies, Malaya and the Continent of Europe. To pay for the food and other imports, they exported goods manufactured in England, transported much of the world's produce in their ships, acted as bankers and money-lenders to other countries. A threat to British power at sea was a threat to all these things.

In the years before the war, the British undoubtedly made mistakes in their foreign policy. But even if they had acted with superhuman wisdom, it is probable that the war could only have been postponed rather than prevented, because Germany was determined to seek more power than Britain or the other Allied countries could in self-defense let her take. When Germany invaded Belgium without warning, the people in Britain were genuinely shocked and sorry for the Belgians. But the more thoughtful among them were equally disturbed for another reason: the conquest of Belgium would give Germany a coast along the English Channel, and would therefore endanger British shipping. The existence of

Belgium was at stake; so was the existence of Britain. So World War I started in August, 1914.

Britain was still suffering from the effects of that war when World War II started twenty-five years later. Between 1914 and 1918, the island kingdom, with a population of 36,500,000 had lost 750,000 men dead. (In the same war, the United States, with a population of 98,000,000 lost 50,000.) Small wonder, then, that in 1939 Britain's leaders were old men or very young men, but rarely middle-aged men with both vigor and experience; most of the leaders who would have been in their forties lay

> "In some corner of a foreign field
> That is forever England."

Small wonder that there were fewer young people growing up; a million women had not become wives or mothers because there weren't enough men for them to marry. Small wonder that the memory of those four grim years still hung over every family; war cripples still limped down every street; peacetime dirigibles were reminders of wartime dirigibles that dropped bombs in the first air raids on London; taxes were still high to cover interest on national debts.

Britain was poorer than she had been before 1914. She had lent large sums to the Continental countries to help them to pay for the war until finally she found it necessary to borrow money from the United States herself. If the Continental countries had been able to repay her after the war, their payments would have more than covered her debt to America. But their lands had been laid waste, their men had been killed, and they could not pay. Consequently, Britain was unable to pay her debts either. The average man did not like not being able to repay money owed to other countries. He would gladly have done anything he could to pay back every penny. But he did not know what he could do about it. He was already trying to raise a family on a wage of about twelve dollars a week, if he had a job, and on next to nothing if he were drawing unemployment insurance. If his children were well fed and decently clothed they were lucky.

So it was that when Germany again showed signs of preparing for war, the people in Britain did not want to fight. They knew what a war would cost. They had had twenty unhappy years since the last one, and another war was certain to leave them poorer in men, in homes, in children, in health, in wealth, in happiness. When war had broken out in Manchuria, they had said, "We won't fight." When Italy attacked Abyssinia, they said, "We won't fight," though by this time a great many of them were getting very worried. When Hitler took over Austria and then Czechoslovakia, they still said, "We don't want to go to war." But they knew, in spite of what they said, that war was coming. They knew they were going to fight, whatever the war might cost. They were going to fight because they believed it was better to be dead, to be crippled, to be poor, than to be a slave to Hitler's Nazis. At the eleventh hour they began to prepare for battle. And when Hitler invaded Poland, whose independence Britain had guaranteed only a few months earlier, Britain kept her promise to the Poles and declared war. The greatest testing time in the history of her people had come.

CHAPTER THIRTEEN

The War Years and After

HALF an hour after the tired and sad voice of Mr. Neville Chamberlain, the Prime Minister, had been heard over the radio telling the people they were at war with Germany, the first air-raid siren sounded over the southern part of England. Millions thought, "This is it." Even while they rushed about turning off the gas that was cooking the Sunday dinner, and gathering their money and private papers, they waited for the sound of the first bombs on London. There had been no time to send most of the children to safer places in the country. Most people had no air-raid shelters. Now mothers picked up their bewildered two- and three-year-olds and thrust them into the dark stuffiness of the clothes closet under the stairs. Ears straining for the roar of the expected thousands of enemy planes, they made a pretense of being gay for the children: "Now Ruth and Betty, we're all going to play a new game. We're going to stay here under the stairs until the policeman blows the big, big whistle, and while we're here we'll each sing a song. Do you want Mummy to start? 'Daisy, Daisy, give me your answer, do! I'm half crazy all for the love of you. . . .' "

But there were no bombs on that bright September Sunday. The bombs were to fall a year later, when Britain, alone of all the states in Western Europe, was still in the fight. Poland, Denmark, Holland, Belgium, Norway, France had fallen prey to the Nazi technique of "Divide and Conquer." Mussolini's Italy had joined in the battle when it seemed certain that there would be no one left for her actually to fight. Sweden, Switzerland, Eire and Portugal were neutral; Spain was technically neutral but in fact Fascist.

Russia was preparing to defend herself against Germany whenever Hitler decided to break the non-aggression pact that formally bound the two countries together. The British Dominions were building munitions plants and training their armies, for, like Britain, they had been caught unprepared. The United States sat watching, alternately booing and shouting, "Come on, Britain, let's go!" And in the Orient, China doggedly retreated in order to fight on, Japanese aggression not yet recognized as part of the world-wide plot against democracy.

The British, awaiting the invasion that might have come at any time after the fall of France, could not retreat. If the worst came to worst and London were conquered, remnants of the government might escape to Canada, there to wage a desperate battle against vastly greater odds. For if Britain had fallen, she would have to have been recaptured before the invasion of the Continent could have been possible. Meanwhile, for the average person in Britain, there was no escape—no friendly shore to which one could sail or row or fly as thousands of Dutch, Belgian and Norwegian refugees were sailing to Britain. Every person in Britain was cornered; so far as he knew, his only chance of getting out of that corner was by fighting his way out personally.

So the country prepared to defend itself. There were not enough weapons; few of the men in the Home Guard owned so much as a shotgun for rabbit hunting. Until revolvers and 22's contributed by Americans arrived in large quantities, the coasts of England were patrolled by men carrying wooden rifles. There was no possibility of stopping German tanks by gunfire, so boys and old men learned how to stop a tank by lying in wait in a roadside hedge or ditch until the enemy came up alongside, and then thrusting a crowbar between the tread and the wheel. Housewives saved empty milk and vinegar bottles to fill with gasoline and use as crude hand grenades. Road signs were removed, all towns rendered anonymous, and even the smallest child knew that if a stranger asked him the way to London, he must invariably answer, "I don't know." No one expected to be able to stop more than one tank or to throw more than one vinegar bottle "Molotov cocktail" before being killed himself, but everyone expected to do his best with his one chance. And through it all, everyone hoped blindly that the sum total of all these personal efforts would add up to a British victory and the downfall of the Nazis.

Meanwhile, the battle for Britain's existence went on at sea. For the British, in this crisis in their history, could not barricade themselves in their island and hope merely to keep out the invader if he came. They had always two enemies—the Nazis and starvation. At one time there was enough food in the country to feed the population for three weeks, no more. Without access to the outer world it was useless even to plow additional land for agriculture since the seeds had to be brought in from outside. And in addition to food, munitions and raw materials had to come from the sister nations of the British Commonwealth, from America, and from the colonies scattered all over the world. Their defense, in turn, became largely the responsibility of the British.

In May, 1940, occurred the magnificent rescue of the bulk of the British Army that had been caught in Belgium and France by the surrender of those two countries. Both the British and the Germans immediately began to call the Dunkirk incident a "miracle." In truth, no one could speak otherwise of the feat of bringing home an army of 335,000 across a notoriously difficult sea passage fifty miles wide, under constant attack from the air, without previous organization of shipping, with amateur crews handling untested and overloaded craft ranging in size from motor launches to paddle-wheel steamers and sailboats to Thames barges, for three heroic days and nights. But Dunkirk was a miracle made by both God and men. To God men gave thanks that the sea was extraordinarily calm so that the little boats that might have foundered in rough weather made the journey back and forth safely. But the miracle of a calm sea would have been of no value had there been no sea-faring folk to sail forth on their adventure, nor could so many of the soldiers have been rescued if they had not maintained perfect order and discipline as they filed out into the water while bombs and machine-gun bullets poured down on them from the skies.

But because Britain was defending not only her shores but her "life-lines" to the outer world, the army that came back from Dunkirk could not stay at home. One of those life-lines led through the Mediterranean to the Red Sea and the Suez Canal to the Indian Ocean, and thence to India, Australia, New Zealand, Hongkong and Singapore. The Nazis were moving toward the south and there was a possibility that the French colonies in Africa might surrender as France had done. The Dunkirk army was therefore re-equipped hastily and at the very time when Britain waited daily for the sound of German tanks in the lanes coming up from the beaches, and when the sixteen-year-olds and the sixties were doing Home Guard drill every night after work, Britain's one trained army was secretly shipped to North Africa to hold the Mediterranean and the Suez Canal.

The action was typical of the leadership of Winston Churchill, who, on May 10th, 1940, had replaced the much deceived Neville Chamberlain. Churchill's passionate hatred of Nazi tyranny, his brilliance as a military strategist with a genius for doing not merely the unexpected but the unheard-of, his robust oratory and his pugnacious high spirits in all adversity, made him a war leader for whom the British gave thanks to Providence all through the grim years of his first term of office as Prime Minister.

The Battle of Britain, which everyone had expected to have to fight in the hedged meadows and on the village greens of southern England was fought instead in the skies above. In July, enemy aircraft were covering Britain on frequent reconnaissance flights. In August the air raids started and for the second time (the first had been when the war broke out) Londoners shipped their children, tagged with baggage labels and herded by their schoolteachers, off to unknown but presumably safer rural areas. By September the

Battle of London had begun, and for fifty-eight successive nights bombs fell on the ancient city. Then the Luftwaffe ranged farther and one by one Coventry, Birmingham, Hull, Liverpool felt its blows.

It was a topsy-turvy war. Soldiers coming home on leave from their safe army camps found their wives and mothers dodging high explosive bombs and putting out incendiaries. Men stationed in Africa and India waited with grim forebodings for news from their civilians in the London battlefront. Only too often their fears were realized and the mail brought a hastily scrawled message: "We had a direct hit on the house night before last; Mum got some bad cuts and lost a lot of blood before they dug her out but she's in hospital now and they say she will be all right. The rest of us are here at the rest centre; we are being taken care of but we don't know what we are going to do."

Apart from the nightly danger and the physical horror of the blitz, life was hard. Supplies of gas and water were often interrupted. Food stores were bombed or closed by time-bombs. Street after street was blocked. Train services and bus routes were disorganized; mail, milk and newspaper deliveries were maintained only by the determination of stubborn men. Like infantry soldiers in the front lines, the average civilian spent sleepless nights under fire and then in the daytime had to allow thrice as long as usual to get to work, to get anything to eat, to come home again. Most people had civilian defense duties to carry out as well. By midwinter they were so tired that they slept anywhere—on the platforms of the subway stations, with trains roaring past their heads every three minutes, in stuffy closets, in damp garden shelters, under their beds —and even in their beds where they were tossed about by every near-hit and where every down-screaming bomb sounded as if it were coming directly toward them.

The time came when the battle for Britain was proving more expensive in aircraft and men than Hitler had expected. Burning oil spread over the waters of the Channel served as a cruel but effective defense against Nazi troops embarking in invasion barges. Thereafter Britain was comparatively free of the fear of war on her own soil, though the air and sea battles continued for four more long and bitter years and each development in bombing technique resulted in more destruction of British resources and more terror for British civilians.

Month after month, the nation labored with all the odds against her. Farmers worked beyond the limits of their strength to plow up more land only to have their best fields requisitioned for use as airdromes or battle-training grounds. Factory managers and labor committees struggled to raise the output of munitions only to hear that entire convoys of ships loaded with their products had been sunk on the way to heavily besieged Malta. Rations of food were barely adequate; most city homes were damp and draughty from bomb damage and the shortage of fuel; rationing of clothes started without warning in June, 1941. People found it painful to recall a past to which there could be no return and unbearable to dream of a future which, by all reasonable thought, could not possibly come to exist because no one could give any logical explanation of how Britain could win the war.

And then the incredible happened. Germany attacked Russia. Guns that were to have been trained on English cities now pointed eastward; bombs which might have fallen on English villages now hurtled down upon the Ukraine. And then relief began to appear from still another quarter. More and more people in the United States were beginning to think that a victorious Hitler ruling all of Europe might be an unpleasant neighbor to have even with an ocean between. Shiploads of food, clothing, medical supplies and equipment, ambulances and mobile canteens for Britain began to leave American ports. Soon the President leased desperately needed American destroyers to the British, who were losing many of their ships in submarine attacks. But the most important measure taken by the United States before the Japanese attack on Pearl Harbor and the German declaration of war against the U. S.

brought her fully into the conflict was the passage of the Lend-Lease Act. Under this Act, the United States supplied goods necessary to Britain and other fighting allies so that they could go on fighting even though they had no dollars with which to pay for them. At the same time, they placed their much smaller resources at the disposal of the United States in situations where doing so would save American lives or equipment. Meanwhile, Britain continued to provide accommodation, military equipment and training for their armies and, if necessary, funds to the governments of occupied countries in order that she might have the assistance of their people in the battle against their conqueror. To pay for all of these things, the British people were taxed at rates almost unbelievable to Americans: there was a 100% sales tax on luxury goods like jewelry, perfumes and fur coats, a 66% tax on many articles for household use. The tax on cigarettes rose to thirty-five cents on a package of twenty, the total cost being forty-seven cents. Above a low level, half a man's income was taken in income tax. Companies had to pay a 100% excess profits tax on profits going above pre-war levels.

When the Japanese attack on Pearl Harbor occurred, the news was received with mingled emotions by the British. They could not help being glad that America's tremendous resources would now be fully used on the side of the Allies. At the same time they were filled with sympathy for the American people for they knew only too well how the Americans were feeling. They were also filled with fears for the hundreds of thousands of their own people stationed in Singapore, Hongkong and at other points in the Orient.

With American participation in the war, the issue was no longer in doubt. In 1942 the first units of the American Army arrived in northern Ireland. Thereafter the stream grew and grew. Finally, there were Americans everywhere, jamming the aisles of the overcrowded trains, filling the buses, the hotels, the skating rinks, the pubs. One Britisher remarked, "Now I know what the American

Indians felt like when the white men came." The American soldiers themselves were well aware of the strain their vast numbers added to the already severe conditions of civilian life.

But time passed, and at El Alamein the first great British victory, heralded as the turning point of the war, was won in North Africa. Then came the African operations starting at Casablanca, and the Italian invasion, while in Britain villages were emptied so that troops could have more battle training. On June 6, 1944 the Americans and the British, with their allies, invaded Europe from the west. A little later, the American Seventh Army struck up through the south of France. The British attempt to end the war by dropping airborne troops at Arnheim failed, and the Allies were dealt a final heavy blow by a Nazi offensive in December. But the advance was broken, and on May 8, 1945 the European war came to an end. Three months later came the collapse of Japan, following the use of the first atomic bombs by the Americans.

World War II had ended. Now to repair what was reparable; to restore what was not wholly lost. The results of the errors of the past were tragically clear; now to lay plans for a future in which those mistakes could be avoided and the final catastrophe of war with atomic weapons could be averted. It was in an atmosphere of high hope that the first session of the General Assembly of the United Nations met in London in January, 1946. And with the establishment of the United Nations and its Security Council, and later, of regional groups such as the North Atlantic Treaty Organization, the pattern of international politics in the post-war world began to appear.

The pattern was disappointing. It had been easier to avoid the recognized mistakes of the past than to foresee all the new problems of the untested future. The machinery of the United Nations seemed hardly strong enough to bear the unexpected strains caused by the shift in Russia's position from that of an ally in the war against Hitler to that of enemy of Western civilization. Trouble broke out in many parts of the world. When, for the first time, there was a show-down between the Western Allies and the Communist group, in Korea, the overwhelming majority of the United Nations troops who fought were American. But Britain, with a national conscription period of two years, had four-fifths of its army abroad, some in Korea, some as Occupation troops in Germany, some in Malaya, some along the ever-vital Suez Canal, some in Singapore and Hongkong, some in Kenya. However fine the threads, there was still a network tying together and keeping clear of Russian domination the places that were traditionally painted red on the map, the old British Empire.

Nevertheless, the average Britisher, faced with the confusion of the post-war world, found it hard to define exactly the role his country was to play on the international stage. Even if, from America and from the Continent, there were appeals for British leadership in creating some sort of European unity, it was hard for some Englishmen to throw aside their inherited sense of apartness from the Continent. Others believed that Britain could, as in the past, play her part in Europe by doing what needed to be done piece-meal rather than by trying to set up a European United States. They were afraid that imposing an American type of government over the extremely varied and self-conscious populations of Europe would lead to demagoguery and dictatorship. None could deny that Britain needed Europe and Europe needed Britain.

Meanwhile, the British looked at their own experiment in international government—the few remaining colonies that were still working their way toward self-government, and the superb sisterhood of independent nations that voluntarily gave their allegiance to the British Crown and they were pleased with what they had done. It was a proud moment for the British when India and Pakistan, given their independence in 1947, remained of their own choice, within the British Commonwealth, along with Australia, New Zealand, South Africa and Canada. Nor was membership in the Commonwealth an empty phrase; when the Prime

Ministers came together in London to celebrate the coronation of Queen Elizabeth II in June, 1953, and then, still moved by the sense of duty, of selflessness and of loyalty to the highest ideals of human behavior which the magnificent ceremony symbolized, sat down at their own conference table to discuss problems of trade, currency control and defense, the atmosphere in which they took up their work encouraged a generosity of outlook and a desire to serve equally all of the peoples concerned. Even when South Africa, convinced that she was right to pursue a racial policy strongly disapproved by the British, decided in 1961 to withdraw from the Commonwealth, there was sadness rather than anger on both sides.

When, during the preparations for celebrating the young queen's coronation, the British called upon their finest poets to write verse, their musicians to compose "garlands of song," their artists and architects to create a fit setting for the ceremony, their craftsmen to spin and weave the silks and to design and embroider the symbolic patterns of the queen's robes, the result was a superb outpouring of talent which bore witness to a whole nation's hope that the event would indeed mark the beginning of a new Elizabethan era. The England of Elizabeth I had triumphed over many difficulties. The England of Elizabeth II was determined to do the same.

Meanwhile, even at home and after eight years of rebuilding, she was short of houses, schools and factories. Meat and other foods were still rationed. Taxes were still abnormally high; only in 1953 did the sales tax on luxury goods drop from 100% to 66%. Critics of the Welfare State established by the Labor government which held office from 1945 to 1951 sometimes feared that Britain's revenue and the Marshall Aid she received from the United States were being spent extravagantly on experiments in socialism. Opinion varied in Britain on such matters as government ownership of certain industries but men of both political parties had the same aim: to make it possible for Britain to get the best out of what she had to work with, whether it was men or materials. Basically, the problem was that wages could not be raised so high in Britain that British goods would become too expensive to be sold abroad, and yet the British workman needed reasonable living conditions if he was to increase production. The need for such things as the National Health Service is easy to understand on this basis. But if the health service achieved relative success, in spite of various flaws, not all the experiments were so fortunate and the crowd in London that cheerfully endured cold wind and rain as it waited to see the Queen's glorious cavalcade returning from Westminster Abbey after the coronation did not need unseasonable weather to remind it that life in the England of Elizabeth II was unlikely to be roses, roses all the way.

Nor was Elizabeth herself likely to find easy her life as the ceremonial head of a family of nations. Her father, George VI, had overcome shyness and the disability of a stammer in order to do well the work which had devolved upon him at his brother's abdication; Elizabeth was bred in the tradition of duty. However, her happy marriage to Prince Philip, Duke of Edinburgh, helped her to carry the burden of public life both as princess and as queen, and the entire Commonwealth rejoiced in the birth of her children: Charles, born in 1948; Anne, born in 1950, and Andrew, born in 1960.

At the time of the coronation in 1953, Britain looked back and took heart from the longer view of her achievements. At that moment her people were sure that they were moving steadily toward a better life than they had ever had. In the years that followed this faith was sometimes shaken. Four million homes were built but there was still a shortage. Meanwhile, the traditionally unrestricted arrival of immigrants from Commonwealth countries, and especially the increasing number of West Indians, (60,000 in 1961) seeking work, created greater tension. Schools improved but England lagged behind many nations in providing enough university places for her young. Full employment was accompanied by labor troubles. Post-war prosperity created surprising problems such as a water shortage; England's drizzle does not provide the vast amounts needed for new manufacturing processes.

Outside Britain, the "cold war" between the Communist and the anti-Communist nations caused many crises. Britain supported the North Atlantic Treaty Organization and the United Nations. In 1956, fearing eventual Communist domination of the Middle East, she, together with France, tried by force to prevent Egypt's taking control of the Suez Canal, but when ordered to do so by the United Nations she immediately withdrew her troops.

But most serious of all her problems, apart from the universal threat of a third world war, was that of earning her living. Britain's decline in economic strength was due less to the loss of her colonies than to the loss of her income from her overseas investments (sold to pay for two wars) and to the loss of her overseas markets. Once an industrial nation selling manufactured goods to undeveloped countries all over the world, she was now an industrial nation trying to sell to other industrial nations, many of them with more raw materials, power and new industrial plants than she had. Somehow she had to overcome her handicaps in order to compete successfully in the nearby European market as well as elsewhere. Step by step the European nations were breaking down barriers that had prevented their buying from each other, selling to each other, working together. A new Europe, perhaps a United States of Europe, was being created. Loyal as she was to the Commonwealth and to that bond between Commonwealth countries that was based on history, sentiment and on mutual advantage in trade, Britain knew that geographically and economically she was also a part of Europe and she had to try to join the nations in the European Common Market who had no outside ties of precisely the same kind. Adjustments had to be made; conflicts of interest between, say, the farmers in France, in New Zealand and in England, had to be kept as small as possible. But change was exciting, and in a competitive world Britain of all nations could not afford to stand still. In the 1960's she was changing fast.

CHAPTER FOURTEEN

The English People and Their Future

WHAT, then, are the English people like? Not what other people sometimes think—the comic-strip pompous Englishman is a figure of fun in England too. Furthermore, the conception that the British (which usually means English) are so wily that any American dealing with them is likely to "lose his shirt" is exactly the same as the British idea of the American business man. In reality, Americans are not as naïve and the British are not as slow as they charge themselves with being.

To accuse Englishmen of hypocrisy or unfair dealings arouses very little feeling on their part; the English know the bad patches in their history better than most Americans and they know quite a number of bad patches in other countries' histories as well. They are realists. They protest vigorously when they think their government is taking unjust measures for their moral sense is keen. But they know, too, how difficult are the problems which face the world today, and they realize that they are bound to make mistakes, however hard they try to be fair to everyone.

There are two impressions of themselves which the English cannot understand at all. The first is the odd combination of the idea already mentioned, that the English are such shrewd bargainers that Americans are putty in their hands, with the idea that at the same time they are slow, old-fashioned and bound by tradition. Clearly they may be one or the other and individual examples of each can be found in England as elsewhere; they cannot be both.

The second impression which bewilders the English is the belief that they cannot see a joke. It is true that their humor differs enough in style from the American for some of their jokes to be incomprehensible to Americans and American jokes to them. But there are fashions in humor, and the "slanging match" now considered typically American was very popular in English "music halls" thirty years ago.

Although no one can make general statements that truly describe all the English as individuals, it is possible to discern certain qualities of the people which run like colored threads through their history, giving it a pattern different from those of other nations. Some of these qualities are inherited from the races which combined to form the modern Englishman. There is the fanciful artistry of the Celt which lives in the magnificent poetry of England, in the national love of pageantry, in the thousand and one waywardnesses of thought or behavior which add to the charm of English daily life. There is the ability to organize and to govern which is so strong that it can operate on the basis of an unwritten Constitution created over a period of seven hundred years, rather than on a written document produced in relatively recent times. That is a skill which may have come down, on the one side, from the Romans, and on the other, from the highly organized Normans, who also established a tradition of excellent craftsmanship in building and engineering. There is a love of the sea which makes it appropriate for American soldiers to refer to all the British as "Limeys" though the nickname was originally given only to British sailors because on their long voyages they drank lime juice to prevent scurvy and other diseases. Most island dwellers love the sea, but the bold traditions of seafaring which once made little Britannia rule the waves came down from King Alfred's sea-going Saxons and the far-ranging Norsemen and Danes.

The English are an easy-going people. They themselves, in their moods of self-criticism which are as sharp as those in which Americans often indulge, say they are too lazy to be anything but easy-going and that therefore their friendly tolerance and calm acceptance of differing attitudes toward life are hardly virtues. The statement is not a fair one for the real cause of English tolerance is the fact that forty-three million people living in an area the size of England have learned from experience that they must be easy-going with each other if they are to get on at all. I have sat in a car in a traffic jam lasting an hour without hearing a single horn blown; English friends laughed at my amazement, saying, "But some people get nervous if you start honking at them, and a tangle like this is going to take long enough to clear up anyway." I have seen people wearing curious clothes—a young man, for instance, who habitually wears a green suit and full-ruffled stock of the eighteenth century —pass unheeded through the streets; people feel that if a person prefers the costume of an earlier century there is no logical reason why he should not wear it every day of his life if he wishes. Even the dogs are trained to bark at strangers only if the strangers' behavior suggests evil intentions.

Such an easy-going manner and habit of tolerance are not easily acquired nor were they characteristic of the English until fairly recent times. They are the result of a lifetime of training in the practice of hiding strong feelings, whether of surprise, joy, impatience or sorrow, lest they embarrass innumerable other people. It is easy to misunderstand such customary suppression of the signs of emotion, and foreigners cannot always be blamed for thinking, however mistakenly, that the British are cold and hard.

With the habit of not showing emotion has developed a feeling that it is in bad taste to give strangers any clue to the secret happenings of private life. English people are often charmed by the American custom of celebrating Mother's Day, but it is hard to imagine them wearing white carnations in honor of their mothers who have died or pink ones for the living. To do so would be to suggest a cause for sympathy or congratulation, and they want neither from strangers. Similarly, there is no custom of hanging gold stars in the window for soldiers killed during a war. It is only inside the house that a visitor may come across the pathetic evidence of a family's sorrow, as I once did in the tidy little parlor of a village postmistress. Everywhere there were vases and ·bowls of artificial flowers—on the mantelpiece, on the piano, on the radio, on the whatnot; but on the table there was a six-penny bunch of brightly colored real anemones in front of a photograph of a smiling young sailor.

"My only son was on the *Hood*," said his mother, matter-of-factly. The great battleship had been lost six months before.

There is another national characteristic which appears to have grown out of the conditions that exist in a country where nearly eight hundred people live per square mile. That is the tendency among many of the English to turn to things for relaxation rather than to people. A celebration, to Americans, means having a party or joining a crowd. There are many Englishmen, on the other hand, whose idea of a perfect celebration is taking a long solitary walk. It is a natural reaction to the constant presence of thousands of people who, by the custom of the country, must be treated courteously and gently at all times. Stop a hurrying Londoner and ask your way; he may think in agony, "I'll miss that train!" and long to wring your neck, but he will pause and answer you politely. No wonder he seeks to spend his leisure in solitude.

Tolerance, a habit of appraising conditions realistically, a sense of humor, kindliness of which courtesy is only one indication—these are all characteristics which ought to make it easy for other people to work with the English so long as they are neither afraid of them nor distressed by the customary coolness of their manner. Has the world anything to fear from the English? What do they want?

They want security. Neither as individuals nor as a nation can the English afford to take chances on losing their livelihood. If a powerful world organization guarantees the life-lines by which Britain obtains employment and food, Britain can relax in her efforts to maintain them within the long-established framework of her Empire and Commonwealth. Until such guarantees exist beyond any shadow of a doubt, the British will defend what remains of their pre-war system.

National security means primarily freedom from fear of war.

There can be no question of the sincerity of the British desire for a permanent peace. In rough proportion to the populations of the two countries, for every American killed or missing in World War II, three British failed to come back to Britain. That was before the atomic bomb. The atomic bomb destroys the security of all the world but of no section of it more surely than of the small crowded British Isles.

Individual security to the British means the certainty of educational opportunity for every child; employment, sufficient food, clothing, good housing, and medical care for every citizen as long as he is able to work; and a pension that will provide these things when he can no longer earn them himself. If, in addition, life can be made easier and gayer by the widespread distribution of automobiles, labor-saving devices and luxury goods, so much the better. People in England would like to have more of these things as much as anyone. But a basic standard of decent living must come first.

It is the determination of the British people to attain a higher basic standard of life than ever before that underlies the recent political history of Britain. For the story that began when King John signed Magna Carta in 1215 is not yet ended. England's history is the story of the common man fighting his way upward from serfdom to individual liberty, political power and economic equality. It is also the story of the growth of the common man's sense of responsibility, for nowhere in the world does the average man realize more clearly than in England the fact that with power comes a heavy burden of duty toward every nation in the world. What Britain's position is to be among world powers, perhaps no one can foretell, but the influence of her people will always fall in favor of the four freedoms for which they themselves led the struggle for so long and for which they are still working. And until all men everywhere are free and secure from fear or want, the rights and the dreams of the common man will be cherished and defended nowhere more warmly than in England, the country in which so much of the liberty that exists in the world first took root.

INDEX